Not Forgetting to Sing

Not Forgetting
To Sing

Nancy E. Robbins

MOODY PRESS • CHICAGO

Oh how can we fight forgetting to sing?
  Are we so doubtful of our morrow
That we must trail a broken wing,
  Make much of sorrow?

A.C.

Preface

We of the Dohnavur Fellowship and Family are very rich in friends who follow our vicissitudes with prayerful interest and concern. Until Amy Carmichael reached the end of her life, her vivid and prolific writing kept these friends well informed about the work which she had begun and which continued for so many years under her inspired leadership. In a class by herself as an author, she had the gift of making people and events come alive for her readers. They found themselves deeply involved in the fortunes of the children, whose whole lives and future had been in jeopardy until in the loving kindness of God they were brought to Dohnavur to find a home here. But her last book about these children was published more than twenty years ago. Yet in spite of this, and even though the news we have sent out has been scanty and inadequate, friends have continued to pray for us. We owe them a debt of eternal gratitude for this loyalty and for their long patience with our default. This book is at last a serious attempt to answer some of their spoken and unspoken questions.

It is however more than that. During the past twenty critical years of radical evolution and change in the new India our God has wonderfully led us on and provided unfailingly for all our needs, material and spiritual. Gratitude to Him impels us to share more widely something of the story of His faithfulness. Having ourselves experienced so much of His amazing goodness, we long to commend our Lord to others.

There is a Tamil proverb which says that one grain of rice is enough to show the quality of the whole pan full. To convey, in this compressed account, the quality and scope of the different parts of so complex a work over so long a period, I must depend on the individual rice-grains. Much is left to the imagination of the discerning reader. This is particularly so with regard to the affairs of the older boys and men, which do not here receive the space and attention they merit. My excuse must be that, writing against time in the midst of a fairly busy life, I have been compelled to draw my material mainly from facts well known to me personally. A more balanced account would have been achieved could it have been written from the viewpoint of one of the leaders. Since however this was not possible I have used my own observations to construct a composite picture. Nevertheless facts have been carefully checked with official records and with the people most concerned, and I trust therefore that the picture as a whole is a true one.

For permission to quote some lines from *The Bhagavadgita* by S. Radhakrishnan I wish to express grateful thanks to Messrs. George Allen & Unwin. The photographs are by past and present members of the Dohnavur Fellowship.

To all who have patiently helped me verify the accuracy of this book's narrative, as well as to those friends who have contributed valuable information, suggestions and criticism, I extend my very warm thanks.

N. E. R.

Dohnavur, India
January, 1967

Contents

Chapter	Page
Preface	vii
Prologue	1
1. WARNING WIRE	11
2. CHILDREN IN PERIL	17
3. JOINING THE FAMILY	25
4. OUTREACH	31
5. CHANGE	40
6. LEADERSHIP	46
7. THE SQUARE	53
8. EDUCATION	58
9. THE END OF AN ERA	66
10. GOD IS FAITHFUL	69
11. PLACE OF LIFE	74
12. CHURCH AFFILIATION AND FINANCE	79
13. OPPORTUNITY	87
14. ON TO HIGHER EDUCATION	93
15. URGENT PROBLEM	100
16. NEW LOOK, NEW PROJECTS	110

17. COVETED OBJECTIVE   118
18. FRUSTRATION   125
19. MATTERS MATRIMONIAL   130
20. CLOUDS AND DARKNESS   136
21. SATISFIED   144
22. REFORM   151
23. RETROSPECT   158
24. CHANGING OUTLOOK, UNCHANGING CHALLENGE   165
25. CHEERFULLY TO CONTINUE   172

Prologue

It had been a hard bleak winter in the industrial midlands of drab war-time England. Morning and evening the waiting-room was thronged to suffocation with a coughing, wheezing crowd intent on procuring "a good bottle of medicine". These people were heartily sick of the war. They had had enough of rationing and queueing and black-out, and now illness was rife among them. The telephone rang incessantly, and our visiting list became fabulously long. We snatched meals when we could and our weekly half-holiday had long ago passed into the realms of myth.

It was the baby who was ill at the vicarage. Glad to escape from the raw damp cold of the outside world, I sat on a low chair by the fire and held her on my knee to examine her. The trouble was relatively slight, and her mother soon began to talk of other things.

"I wonder if you would care to come to a missionary meeting on Monday afternoon?" she asked.

In my mind's eye I saw a queue outside the surgery, and a visiting list as long as my arm, and wanted to say "What a hope!"

All the same I was interested. During my five years or so of work in that practice no-one had ever invited me to a missionary meeting before.

"Who is your speaker?" I asked.

"Miss Gibson of the Dohnavur Fellowship in South India," came the reply.

Dohnavur again! What could this mean? I was so surprised that for a second the baby was forgotten and in imminent danger of being dropped.

Recovering myself I told my little patient's mother that I would come to her meeting if I had time, but that I thought this to be very unlikely. My thoughts were in a turmoil as I drove off to the next call on that chilly afternoon.

Only a week or two earlier a friend, to whom I owed much for her sterling Christian life and example, had written one of her rare letters.

"Have you quite given up the thought of missionary service in India?" she asked. It appeared that she always prayed for me on Tuesdays, and that she also prayed regularly for the work of the Dohnavur Fellowship on that day. Dohnavur needed a woman doctor, and she knew that years before I had believed myself called to India. Now she had suddenly felt strongly constrained to ask God to let me be the answer to her prayers for Dohnavur in this respect, and to tell me of the request.

I had not given up the thought of missionary service; indeed I had been thinking much of it again lately. Home circumstances, illness, the adverse advice of doctors expert in tropical matters, and war; all had combined to block my red-hot plans for leaving for the mission-field soon after qualifying. Yet in the last few months I had become increasingly sure that God did not intend me to settle down to general practice in Britain for the rest of my life. I would have chosen something independent and adventurous for myself however, and the life of a large community did not appeal. I wrote to my friend by return of post, feeling faintly indignant at her "interference", to say unequivocally that I felt Dohnavur was not for me. I tried then to forget the suggestion. But it haunted me. I could not dismiss it from my mind.

Was it then God Himself who was bringing Dohnavur to my notice again so soon? I asked Him to make it possible for me to go to that meeting if He had something to say to me through it —and felt I was asking for a miracle. I hoped I would not be able to make it, and that then I might be allowed to put Dohnavur right out of my mind and make different plans for my future. But no, I could not escape the sense that God was speaking to me. And who, having once heard the voice of the Shepherd, does not want to hear that voice again? It was all very confusing.

Monday came. The 'phone was strangely silent. Morning surgery passed uneventfully, and when I had seen the last patient I went to enquire from the receptionist what new calls had come in during the morning. She was obviously puzzled. "Only *two* new calls today, Doctor," she said.

Much to my embarrassment I arrived a minute or two late at the meeting that afternoon, and had to sit right under the speaker's eye. It was a most disturbing hour. I had read books about Dohnavur, and did not hear much that was new to me; but the conviction grew that God was indeed speaking through the co-incidences of the last few weeks.

I decided I had better reread *Gold Cord*, the book in which Amy Carmichael has written the story of the beginnings of her rescue work for children, and of the growth of the Dohnavur Fellowship. Years before I had given a copy to the friend of the unwelcome letter. Now I came down off my high horse, and wrote asking her if she would mind lending it to me, as, after all, I found I needed to know more about the work of which it told.

My reading was mostly done late at night. The lull in the work of the practice had lasted for only one day. The rush continued for several weeks more.

Amy Carmichael's writing had made no specially strong appeal to me in the past. Now it seemed that *Gold Cord* must have been written entirely for me. The danger to the children of whom she wrote became real and urgent. It was intolerable to think of them caught up in a system designed, whether intentionally or not, to lead them into a life of degradation and sordid sin, a life from which escape seemed virtually impossible. That the system was ostensibly a religious one based on the ancient temples made it seem the more sinister. The work of rescuing them from such a fate seemed eminently worthwhile. It was clear however that this was no mere philanthropic social venture based on a warm-hearted humanitarian feeling for little children. Amy Carmichael was extremely self-effacing in her writing, but quite obviously she was a woman of unusual gifts and ability. With a natural aptitude for languages and for entering into Indian thought and culture, she had early built up a most successful evangelistic work in the Tamil country in association with one of the great established missions. Yet she had willingly laid this down in order to look after a lot of delicate babies and a family of growing children, with only a handful of helpers and no mission backing. Many of her personal friends and much of the Christian world in general had been critical of her action, and at the outset she had known loneliness and discouragement. Undaunted she had gone steadfastly on in what, she had no doubt at all, was the task that God Himself had entrusted to her. The driving power in her life was her whole-hearted love for the Lord Jesus, inexorably translated into obedience to His lightest wish. The work for the children involved constant personal sacrifice, but in them she saw potential witnesses for Christ in the India of the future. Nothing was too costly to give if only they might be fitly trained for His service. Such training could be no mere theory impersonally applied. It had to be a long labour of love for each individual that involved identification with them in their life, their joys and their sorrows. This involvement in the lives of others inevitably brings exposure to deep hurt should any fall into sin or come short of the goal.

Fellow workers who joined Miss Carmichael would naturally expect to participate in all this right up to the hilt. I had thought of the community as being sheltered and spiritually enervating but what I read presented a compelling challenge to total commitment to Jesus Christ. It meant, too, commitment to one another in His service. Amy Carmichael found these two concepts epitomised in the story told in I Chronicles 11 of David's three mighty men who, regardless of personal danger, broke through the enemy lines to draw water from the well in Bethlehem just because their master had expressed a desire for it. This showed her the lines on which to pray for the Fellowship. She wrote: "*To love our Captain so* makes for perfect comradeship. 'And the three brake through.' They knew that they could count on one another without reserve to the end."

Workers and children all lived together as a family. All had some practical contribution to make to the life of the Family and of the countryside, and service of this practical kind afforded occasion for witness by word as well as by life.

The work was not sponsored or guaranteed by any overseas organisation or society. No appeal was made for funds. The needs of the Family were made known only to God, and the supplies He had sent had always been enough.

With great trepidation I read what was written concerning the kind of recruits needed. They must be "eager, joyfully eager to do anything, anywhere, anywhen, for love of their Lord." There followed a quotation from the Letters of Père Didon: "I do not want people," he had said, "who come to me under certain reservations. In battle you need soldiers who fear nothing." Miss Carmichael went on to explain how as years went by she was led to pray that prospective candidates might be proved and tested in every possible way at the home end before they set out. She wanted only those to join the work who were so sure of God's call that no calamitous happening, no fear or discouragement could make them abandon it.

By the time I had got to the end of the book my world had been turned upside down. I was no longer asking myself whether I was willing to go, but whether God could possibly be willing to send and use one such as I knew myself to be. As one night I reviewed my life on my knees, I thought it quite impossible that He could ever do so. I could only ask Him that He would make me whatever He wanted me to be, and do with me what He would. At length I turned to the *Daily Light* portion for that evening and was startled by words that I recognised as being His word to me. "The LORD is with thee . . . go in this thy might."

It seemed strange the next morning that the household, absorbed as usual in the mundane business of porridge and the daily papers, did not see the golden radiance on the fresh white pear blossom against the clear spring sky. God had spoken, and for me the day was filled with a shining beauty I have never forgotten.

There was nothing but the light of common day on the practical details involved in telling my family and partner in practice of the proposed step, and then formally offering to the Dohnavur Fellowship. As the news got around there were plenty of people to tell me what a fool I was to leave a good job with a steady income at such a time. India was in the throes of her historic struggle for independence. The days of missionaries, especially of British ones in India, were, I was assured, numbered. It might well be impossible to get back into medical practice in England, once having left it.

Was all this talk, I wondered, the testing for which Amy Carmichael would now be praying on my behalf?

It was wonderful therefore to experience the Lord's powerful intervention in the long obsolete war-time formalities of those days. Release by the Medical War Committee was, I was assured, as likely to be granted just then as a request for the moon. It was in fact granted at once, because the local chairman "happened" to remember a remark of my partner's, made "by chance" more than five years before, to the effect that the woman doctor about to join his practice might not stay long, as she hoped to be a missionary. "This is not a sudden whim," he told his committee. "She has served in the district all through the war years, and she ought to be released now." On the strength of this decision an Exit Permit was granted, and then I was required by the emigration authorities to sign an undertaking that I would accept, at twenty-four hours' notice, any offer made to me of a passage to India.

It was at this point that I was informed by long-distance telephone that my father had been seriously injured in a road accident and was in hospital. My partner kindly set me free at once, and I drove towards London wondering what lay ahead. My brave mother was obviously relieved to see me walk into the house. When I saw my father, I felt sure he was dying. He was confused and only semi-conscious, but his rambling, disjointed talk made one thing clear. Although he had done nothing to prevent my going to India, he was convinced the whole thing was a big mistake.

In the days that followed, friends and relatives understandably assumed that I would now abandon my folly and settle in England. The grief of parting might be enough, they suggested, to loosen

my father's feeble hold on life altogether. I was terribly afraid
it might.

What if my twenty-four hours' sailing notice were to come
now?

"Remember the word unto Thy servant upon which Thou hast
caused me to hope," was the cry of my heart to God. That lighted
day in March seemed now very far removed from these present
weeks of bewilderment and darkness. Yet perhaps it is not possible to know the depths of the Lord's love until one has had
reason to prove Him as the God of all comfort. Enduring bonds
of fellowship are forged at such a time, and I was upheld by the
prayers of comrades in Dohnavur whom I was yet to meet.

My worst fears proved groundless. My father was on the way to
recovery and at home when my passage was granted. He was
permanently crippled, but he lived for another fourteen years.
By God's goodness I was on furlough during his last months on
earth and able to help him through his final illness.

Just about a year after receiving the letter that so disturbed my
peace of mind, I set sail from Liverpool to come to India. It was
a dreary grey day in January 1946 and an icily penetrating east
wind was blowing. The passport officials seemed endlessly slow
in dealing with the long queue of passengers, but at last we were
all aboard. We finally left England sometime after midnight.

Nearly three weeks later, on a morning of brilliant sunshine, the
ship steamed slowly into Bombay harbour. One moment the silver
sea was empty, shimmering in a dazzling heat haze. The next it
was covered with myriads of dancing red sails, and then there was
the Gateway of India, noise, bustle, and a kaleidoscope of colour.

The railway journey from Bombay was fascinating, but it was
also slow and dusty and very hot. Up into the Western Ghats it
led, out across the Deccan plateau and down to Madras; then
south again through the whole length of Tamil-nad, and on

towards India's southernmost limit. On the third night of this
journey I was left alone. Friends from the ship with whom I had
set out had already left the Express and were by now at their
destinations. The train shrieked and swayed its way onward
through the darkness, the noise it made rivalled only by the
cacophony of platform sounds at each stop. Food and coffee and
sweetmeat vendors cried their wares on every note of the scale,
passengers bawled as they struggled for places on the over-full
train, coolies clamoured for exorbitant tips, gongs clanged and
whistles blew. There were many sounds that I could not interpret,
and smells that I could not identify. At one point the train halted
in a seemingly desolate spot and gently let off steam. I could see
its lights reflected in water on either side of the line. Could these
be flooded rice-fields? And could that noise like the bubbling of a
thousand pans of porridge really be made by frogs? There was
no-one to tell me.

The next afternoon I had a very kind welcome on Tirunelveli
station from the folk who had come out by car the thirty miles to
meet me. They seemed strangely preoccupied with the need to
reach Dohnavur by four o'clock. Idly I wondered why. When you
have been travelling continuously for seven thousand miles you
might surely be forgiven for being a few moments late for tea?
We rattled noisily over dusty roads with pigs, cows and children
scattering before us. Fat water buffaloes, ignoring the urgent pleas
of our horn, lumbered heavily across our tracks to stand and
survey us long and mournfully as we screeched to a standstill.
Ahead the mountains rose to a final impressive bastion before
tumbling into foothills that mark the very limit of India.

As we neared them the countryside became beautiful with
standing water and green paddy fields, and the road was shaded by
enormous spreading trees. Suddenly between these the distant red
roofs of Dohnavur appeared, and in no time we were pausing

briefly at the hospital gate to greet some of the staff. Then on we drove past work-shops, a playing-field, school buildings, a clock-tower, and round a last corner between little houses half hidden among the trees to an open space in front of the House of Prayer. There, waiting expectantly, were crowds of gay children and adults in bright saris. The tinies were waving flags and some-where bells were pealing. The car drew up, children with flowers in their hair ran forward to take my hand and lead me inside. I had not for one moment expected a welcome like this, and was almost overwhelmed by impressions of light, colour and then joyful song.

O God of stars and flowers, forgive our blindness;
No dream of night had dared what Thou hast wrought.
New every morning is Thy loving-kindness,
Far, far above what we have asked or thought.

So under every sky our alleluia,
With flowers of morning and with stars of night,
Shall praise Thee, O Lord Jesus, Alleluia,
Till Thou shalt fold all shadows up in light.

1

Warning Wire

"Baby girl for disposal."

It was a stifling evening in May 1946, the hottest month of the year. Those members of the Fellowship who were not on holiday in the nearby hills were startled at the wording of the reply-paid telegram which was read out to them at dinner time. This was a matter calling for urgent prayer and quick action, but alas, the sender of the telegram, whose name was an all too common one, had omitted to telegraph an address. Beyond the fact that the wire had been handed in to a Madras post-office there was no clue to her whereabouts or that of the baby. As far as we were concerned, that seemed to be that.

Alison Wiggins left the main bungalow where we assemble for meals and meetings and made her way to her house. She prepared for bed and turned in, but not to sleep. All night long she tossed restlessly, thinking of the baby girl whose "disposal" was so urgent. What, she wondered, would be done with her when the telegram brought no reply? She was haunted by the thought of the big temples in Madras, and of the staff of women associated with them who were always on the look-out for likely little ones to "adopt" and train up in their own profession as servants of the gods.

In the morning, still unable to settle peacefully to anything, Alison went to see Dr. May Powell.

"Are you going to do anything about that telegram?" she demanded.

May explained that she had felt nothing was possible in the circumstances. Then, seeing how deeply Alison was feeling she added, "If you are sure the Lord is telling you to do something about it, why not arrange to travel to Madras with Philip England tomorrow? Even if you can't trace this baby, you could bring back the one that is waiting for an escort at the home of those other friends."

Alison needed no second bidding. Quickly she set about making the necessary arrangements, which included finding an Indian fellow worker to go with her as a companion.

Philip was leaving for a long-overdue furlough, and it was a great advantage to have his assistance on the four-hundred-mile journey. On arrival in Madras, he made enquiries about the telegram, located the post-office from which it had been sent, and from there was able to trace the sender to a mission hospital.

Through the help of an Indian friend of the hospital it was soon learned from the staff that a patient having the same name as the one telegraphed had left the wards a few days earlier. They were able to give him her address, which was in a large town fully an hour's journey out of the city.

Nothing daunted, Alison caught a train for this town early the next morning. She found the house quite easily and walked in and introduced herself. The occupants were a prosperous elderly couple, with a grown-up son.

"I have come from Dohnavur," she explained. "You sent a telegram about a baby. I have come for it."

The couple looked at one another in obvious consternation. "Oh, but you did not reply," they said.

"No," agreed Alison. "You forgot to telegraph your address, so we couldn't."

There was dismay on their faces. Obviously these people had not, until that moment, realised their omission. Now its significance dawned upon them.

They proceeded to tell her about the baby, whose mother, a trained nurse, was in fact there in the house. She had been working in a hospital in Iraq on a war-time assignment, and while there had got into trouble. A fellow nurse, the daughter of the folk in whose house she was now staying, had brought her back to India where her baby had been born in the mission hospital to which Alison had traced her. She was, they said, friendless and without relatives who could help her, and so must earn her own living and could not keep her child. The lady of the house vaguely remembered visiting Dohnavur many years before, when she herself was still a girl. She it was who had suggested sending the telegram. When no reply came they were at their wits' end. They did not want to be seen leaving the hospital with the baby, and so in desperation they gave her to "a woman who was working around the place, and who seemed glad to have her".

Alison's heart sank. What kind of woman was this, she wondered?

That morning God had given her a promise. Now that the prospect of saving the little girl from a fate worse than death seemed so remote Alison staked everything upon His word.

"Before I set out to come here this morning," she said, "God gave me a verse of scripture. It was this: 'Be ye steadfast, unmoveable, always abounding in the work of the Lord forasmuch as

ye know that your labour is *not in vain in the Lord.*' I believe God
means to give me that baby."

Her listeners were impressed, and declared their willingness
to help. They had sent the wire, they said, because they wanted
the child brought up a Christian.

"Our son shall go back with you," they proposed. "He knows
the woman who took the child. He saw her at the hospital."

With the thermometer standing at 105° F in the shade, Alison
toiled back into the city of Madras, and to the hospital. The
young man enquired there for the woman who had taken the baby,
and once again the staff were helpful. They gave him her address.

A long bus ride brought the two of them to a quarter of the
city where there was an open square of houses, flanked on one
side by a massive Hindu temple with a great towering *gopuram*
shadowing its dark entrance. Sensing the atmosphere of the place,
Alison began to realise why the Lord had led her on with such a
sense of urgency in her quest for this particular child.

They had scarcely alighted from the bus when the young man
saw her. There she stood, the woman they had come to find! He
spoke to her in low rapid Tamil which Alison was unable to
follow. Without demur, "I will bring the child," she replied,
and began to walk away.

Alison started to follow but the woman rounded upon her
angrily. "Don't you come to my street," she shouted.

In a few moments she returned carrying a fragile exhausted-
looking infant, whom she put into Alison's arms. Immediately a
crowd of men, fair-skinned and bare to the waist but wearing over
their shoulders the sacred thread of the twice-born, began to
gather from the surrounding houses. They were Brahmans connected with the temple and its ceremonies, and the talk was
menacing and hostile. "What does the white woman want with
that baby?" one of them exclaimed.

Just as it seemed that a difficult situation might develop a bus drove into and round the square, and drew up beside Alison. She got in, and found it was routed to pass by the very house where she and her companion were staying with missionary friends. Squeezing herself into a seat between two women, she wrapped the baby in a piece of cotton material the same colour as her own sari. There it lay still and quiet in her lap unnoticed by anyone throughout the long crowded journey.

.   .   .

The above is one story among many. Here is another from six months later.

It was November 1946 and Lotus was returning home after a day's work. Wending her way through the busy streets of the city where she lived, she noticed walking ahead of her a young woman with a small girl clinging desperately to her sari. The woman was clearly in distress and was weeping so uncontrollably that, coming alongside, Lotus felt constrained to ask her kindly if she needed any help. At first the sobbing woman could say nothing, but as Lotus persisted in her efforts to comfort her, she began to tell her story.

She belonged to a family in which it had long been the custom to dedicate the eldest daughter in each generation to Mari-amman, the "Destroying Mother" or goddess of small-pox, in a certain temple in the city to which she had now come. She knew something of what this dedication would mean to her child, whom she dearly loved, but she could see no escape from it. Her family had sent her with instructions to leave the child at the temple and return. She dared not disobey them, more especially as her husband had died two months earlier and so she was without his help, alone and dependent on them. She did not know how to face the parting, with all that it implied. It would have been different had she thought the child would be loved and

kindly treated, but to be a "servant of the gods"—the prospect
was appalling.

Lotus possessed an understanding heart. She had been brought
up in Dohnavur as a child, and was now happily married with
children of her own. She invited the woman and her little
daughter to come home with her and have something to eat.
While they enjoyed their meal she told them something about her
own childhood, and the loving home in which she had spent it.
Her guest listened eagerly, asking many questions. When it was
suggested that she might send her own little girl to that same
home, she was overcome with relief. Her heart leapt at the
proposal. Here was a welcome alternative to the fate she had
foreseen for her child. Already reconciled to the parting, she
returned alone to her village satisfied, while Lotus travelled to
Dohnavur bringing the forlorn little three-year-old to her new
home.

2

Children in Peril

What lay behind the stories just recounted?

Early in 1947, as a comparatively new recruit, I was able to see for myself just a little of the system in which these two children had so nearly become entangled.

With Indian companions I was staying not far from Dohnavur in a small temple town. An important local Hindu festival was in progress. Night and day for more than a week the throbbing of drums and the thin piercing sound of pipes became an integral part of life. Gorgeously draped palanquins bearing idols heavily gar-landed were carried at all hours shoulder high through the streets. Crowds drifted about the town, the women with flowers in their hair and dressed in their gayest clothes. All were eager to see what was to be seen and to win whatever merit might, for a considera-tion, be gained at such a festival. Children happily gorged them-selves on the rich sweetmeats offered for sale at roadside stalls, and pestered their parents to buy them balloons and simple toys. The air was oppressive with the scent of jasmine and roses, while

incense mingled its aroma with the stench of garbage and the
smells of cattle and perspiring humanity. Among the festive
masses were a few truly devout and wistful pilgrims who
anxiously prostrated themselves in the dust before each idol, and,
whenever he appeared, before the *Jeer-swami* or high priest of the
central shrine. For them the cheap and tawdry aspects of the
festival held no attraction. They were the seekers. Yes, but what,
one asked oneself, or whom, were they seeking?

One day a small child told us with bated breath, "Tonight the
dasis will be dancing."

Hindu friends who thought we might like to see this perform-
ance made arrangements for us to watch from the dark, secluded
verandah of a house at the corner of the temple street. The whole
street was lighted by flares and was packed to suffocation point
with men. I learned later that no woman who valued her reputation
would dream of being seen out at such a time.

Presently the eagerly awaited procession appeared. At its head
walked the temple elephant, its dignified brow painted with a
lurid red-and-white Vaishnava sign proclaiming its servitude to
Vishnu the third god of the Hindu triad. It passed on and was
followed by a group of the temple musicians; and then the sacred
palanquin itself advanced, borne shoulder high by teams of pant-
ing, sweating men. On it swayed the glittering gold-plated idol
of Hanuman the monkey god, who was the special object of
veneration that night. Almost opposite the house where we were
concealed the bearers rested their burden and paused for breath.
Flares threw into relief the crouched ape-like figure of the idol.
They revealed too the expressions of absorbed interest on the faces
of the waiting crowd and cast weird flickering shadows on the
huge vertical red stripes that adorned the white temple walls
behind.

Into the space cleared before the god there now stepped forth a *dasi*, a beautiful young girl, lavishly dressed, her jewels glinting in the torches' fitful glare. To the sound of pipes and the exotic rhythms of a *mirudhangam* she began a ritual dance. It was lively and graceful in its way, but full of sickeningly meaningful gestures. How intently her every posture was watched by the street full of jostling, sweating men as they craned to get a better view! The dance of course had a religious significance which largely escaped me, but its erotic character was plain for all to see. I shall not easily forget the scene.

It was a day or two later that, as I walked through the town, a little girl whom I did not know ran up and took my hand. She gave me a pressing invitation to come with her into the temple courtyard to see the elephant being fed. Not satisfied with this, she dragged me off next to see her home.

All unsuspecting I followed my attractive little hostess, to find when I reached there that, to my surprise and dismay, I had been led into the *dasis'* house. Very naturally these women were not at all pleased to see me there. As soon as courtesy permitted I excused myself and left, but not before I had been struck by the quite unusual number of men hanging around that house of ill-repute.

Presumably my small friend was being trained to participate in the life of that group of *devadasis*. If so she must already have learned many of the songs and dances that she would need to use in her future life. By her early teens or maybe sooner she would go through her initiation ceremony of marriage to the god, and from then on she would be compelled to live the life of a prostitute under the specious guise of divine service.

Let it be said at once that in that spring of 1947, on the eve of India's Independence, the social sense of the nation was very much awake to these wrongs. Already her reformers were actively framing legislation designed to abolish the Devadasi System.

Mahatma Gandhi himself had led the way in outspoken criticism of the system, deploring it as a grave social evil, discreditable to the whole of Hindu philosophy. At the time here described, however, no major reforms had yet been achieved.

The facts have never been in dispute. As recently as 1962 for example an enquiry into the causes of prostitution in Bombay State was instituted by the Association for Moral and Social Hygiene in that State. It revealed that the Devadasi System was still, even at that late date, an important cause of this and of its accompanying traffic in small children. The following is an extract from the Association's published report:

"The term Devadasis literally means servants (slaves) of God and perhaps originally denoted a class of women who gave themselves to a life of religious service and austerities . . . The custom of dedicating girls to Hindu temples came into practice . . . about the third century A.D., when it was considered very rewarding for (the soul of) a person seeking religious merit to purchase girls and dedicate them to the temples, as advocated in the *Puranas*.* A dedicated girl is considered to be a bride of the god of the temple and therefore she is barred from marrying . . .

"The girls so dedicated were assigned certain duties to be performed at the temples, such as fanning the deities and cleaning and lighting the oil lamps, but their major function had been singing and dancing at the temple ceremonies. In return for their services they received *Inama* lands† and cash allowances out of the rich endowments of the temples. These material benefits tempted needy parents to dedicate their daughters to prosperous temples. The young women, thus forced into a life that offered no opportunity for the fulfilment of their natural

* Ancient Hindu philosophical writings.
† Gift lands free from tax.

urges and worldly desires, could be easily induced to lead an immoral life by their exploiters."

The report goes on to point out that the girls themselves were not party to their own dedication.

"Usually parents, guardians or relatives take an irrevocable vow while the girl is still in infancy or childhood that she shall be dedicated . . . either in order to keep up the tradition of dedicating at least one daughter of the family, or as a bargain against the granting of a favour, often a trivial one at that."*

They often gave the child to the temple soon after birth, and the ceremony of "marriage to the god", which heralded initiation into all aspects of life as a *dasi*, took place as soon as adolescence was reached. The investigators summarised their findings on this subject by saying:

"Prostitution is so much and so long associated with the Devadasis that they now almost claim it as their traditional profession."

But whatever may have been true in Bombay State in 1962, it is certain that by that date in the State of Madras the Devadasi System was no longer an important cause of prostitution and of the traffic in small children. The picture given by Punekar and Rao in this report corresponds more nearly to the situation here twenty or so years earlier, that is to say, around the time when the events just recorded took place.

Connected as it was with the temple and their ritual, the role of the *devadasi* enjoyed the ancient sanction of religion, while the classical dances she was taught to perform possessed also a strong cultural and aesthetic appeal. Perhaps there was once a time when it was connected exclusively with religious devotion and marked by nothing but piety and propriety, but throughout recent cen-

* S. D. Punekar, M.A., Ph.D. and Kamala Rao, Lit.B., Dip.S.S.A., *Report of the Association for Moral and Social Hygiene*, Bombay, 1962.

turies it has certainly come to afford a cloak for license and moral degradation.* Small wonder then that public moral sense has led serious men and women to cry out for a change, and that today social reform has proceeded, slowly but inexorably, towards effective legal abolition of the whole system with its attendant ills.

It was to save little girls from this kind of exploitation that in 1901, while the system was yet at its height, Amy Carmichael knew herself commissioned of God. She became in due course *Amma* (that is Mother) to many of these children, and as Amma we still think of her.

It must of course be added that, as might be expected, the temples were by no means the only source of moral danger to small unprotected children.

At the end of 1946 an Indian film company was engaged in making a picture featuring a story of one of the gods. According to the legend this god, during a temporary sojourn on earth, paid a visit to a particular woman. Caught in the house on her husband's arrival, he eluded him, the story goes, by quickly transforming himself into a small infant.

For this episode of the film a baby was needed, and a mother who found herself in dire and urgent straits of some kind was persuaded to sell her little daughter for the purpose. The baby in the story was *very* small. Consequently this helpless living child was deliberately kept half-starved in order that she should not grow bigger for as long as it took to prepare and shoot the scene in which she appeared. A magistrate who lived and worked in the city where this took place came to hear about it, removed the baby from the cinema company, and brought her to us.

As is well known, India has the third largest cinema industry in the world. Films are produced to the tune of some three hundred

* See M. Monier-Williams, *Brahmanism and Hinduism*, London, 1891, p. 451.

a year in seven or more languages.* Some have modern stories showing western influence. Others re-enact the old legends of the gods, with their often equally dubious morality. Most are acknowledged to be of poor creative quality with monotonously stereotyped themes.† Yet they are watched by an estimated two million a day, very many of whom go avidly back to see the same salacious scenes over and over again.

In the making of these films small children of various ages, both boys and girls, are often in demand. They may be hired for a wage, but if instead they are taken over outright by the company their fate is a sad one indeed. Their film career is often very short, and when their acting is no longer financially rewarding they tend to be abandoned without proper care or protection. Even if advantage has not already been taken of their youth and ignorance before they leave cinema employ, it is likely that the only means of livelihood open to them afterwards will be the life of the streets.

The little girl brought to us by the magistrate was an extreme case. Had she stayed much longer with the cinema people it is very doubtful whether she would have survived to be exposed to this kind of danger. It took her a long time to secure a grip on life after her gruelling experience.

But there were then, and we believe still are, many other little children liable to this and similar kinds of exploitation. For example little boys were often in demand to take child parts in the age-old religious drama of the larger Hindu temples, a form of entertainment which the cinema has now largely superseded. It was the discovery of this considerable peril to young lives which in 1918 led Amy Carmichael to provide also a refuge and a home for little boys at Dohnavur. Nor was this all, for certain people too, mainly Muslims from a neighbouring state, made a business

* *"Times of India" Directory and Year Book*, 1965–66, p. 173.
† S. C. Sarkar, *Hindustan Year-Book*, Calcutta, 1959, pp. 528f.

of procuring small boys for directly immoral purposes, and there is some evidence that this traffic still continues. By these and other less notorious means are innocent children exposed to the desolate life of the morally abused and outcast.

The finding and rescuing of such children is, of course, only the first round in a long contest with the enemy, who once had counted them his prey. The subsequent battle for their souls is often fierce and discouraging, but with us is the One who said: "The prey of the terrible shall be delivered; for I will contend with him that contendeth with thee, and I will save thy children."

3

Joining the Family

Alison's adventures were not over when she alighted from the bus
with her precious charge and rejoined her missionary friends in
their home. She had had an exhausting day of heat, dust and tension. Now there was only just time for a much-needed bath and a
meal before it would be necessary to set out for Egmore Station
and the Night Express to Tirunelveli. The other baby who had
been waiting for an escort was collected. Then, just at the last
moment, an Indian woman friend turned up with still another
little girl destined for Dohnavur.

When Alison and her companion arrived with the three babies
at the railway station, they found a scene of noisy confusion.
Crowds were fighting and struggling to board the third-class
section of the Express through doors and windows. Some fortunate
possessors of tickets were reselling them at a fantastic profit. There
was no seat left in the upper-class coaches either, and the booking
clerk said that all seats in express trains to Tirunelveli were
booked for the next three days.

There was nothing for it but to abandon the journey for that night and return to their friends. The prospect of some hours of undisturbed sleep was very welcome, and was made possible because these friends kindly arranged for the night care of the babies.

Next day the small party managed to find a place on a slow passenger train, one that panted wearily from station to station and took twenty-seven hours to complete the four-hundred-mile journey. Unfortunately Alison's companion was so badly afflicted with travel sickness as to be of little help with the babies. It seemed that whenever two of these were quiet the third needed attention, and the journey was one long round of preparing and giving bottles, and changing nappies. It was not easy to buy provisions on the way, and there were all the usual accompaniments of noise, heat, dust and congestion. Even the worst journeys come to an end however, and at last they arrived triumphantly in Dohnavur.

The advent of a new baby was by no means unusual, but never failed to cause a pleasurable stir of excitement throughout the big Family. The news was passed from mouth to mouth.

"A new baby."

"*Three* new babies!"

Three? This *was* exceptional. Was it perhaps a story that grew in the telling? No, it was in fact true!

The first thing to be done was to take the little ones to Amma's room. Old, ill and tired though she might be, her face would be alight with gratitude to the Lord who had saved yet more children from a tragic fate and entrusted them to us to be trained for Him. She would take each baby in her arms, and lovingly commit the little life with all its potentialities to Him. Nor did she forget to pray for those who would have a share in the extra work and added responsibilities involved with the coming of each new child.

Her prayers were brief and practical and gave one the feeling that God was very near.

Amma chose Tamil names for the three little girls, each with the word "pearl" in it. The baby whom Alison had worked so hard to find was called "Garland of Pearls". In Roman characters the Tamil word would look bizarre, and the English translation, you will agree, is long and clumsy. For the purposes of this book, therefore, we shall call her Meenila.

Alison's next duty was to allocate each little one to the *Accal* or older Sister in the Family who would mother her during the ensuing months. There were three of these Accals who were giving their whole lives to the care of tiny babies. All of them were middle-aged by this time and all had themselves been brought up in Dohnavur.

Meenila went to the care of Sellachie* who gave her the warmest of welcomes. In next to no time she was bathed and fed and peacefully sleeping in the little white cloth hammock slung for her from the rafters. The fact that this added one more to the seven or eight other babies of under one year that Sellachie was already caring for did not perturb her in the least. Each new child brought more work, but it brought, too, added joy. What matter a few more broken nights? She had had plenty in her time, and sleep was not everything.

During the next couple of years I was destined to become well acquainted with Meenila and her companions in the *Bala Stala* (literally, Babies' Place) as their domain was called. As a respite from language study I sometimes did odd jobs there, and later, while Alison was on furlough, I took on the general supervision of this department. There were six nurseries in all. Three were for tiny babies, and three for those who had reached the

* Her story is told in Chapter XXX of Amy Carmichael's *Windows*, London, S.P.C.K., 1937.

toddling stage. All told there were about fifty children there.

Meenila settled down well and thrived during her infancy. Some of her contemporaries were frail and delicate. Some were seriously under-nourished or diseased before they ever came to us, and these often gave a great deal of anxiety during their early years. Such children made great demands on those who cared for them. I noticed that some babies who had been doing well lost weight and were disturbed emotionally by the change of personal care when they moved up from the tinies' to the toddlers' nurseries. Altogether they seemed much more vulnerable and difficult to rear than children of comparable ages of whom I had had experience in the homeland.

When I went to inspect their weight charts and enquire into their general well-being I enjoyed playing with them and, as I got to know them individually, speculating on their future. They were all so different. There was a humorist who was always perpetrating jokes on other people and chuckling gleefully at the results. Meenila herself was a lively youngster, never at a loss for interesting occupation, and very quick in all her movements. In sharp contrast one of her friends always looked tired and faintly bored, as though, having savoured life for more than a year, she had convinced herself that it was all emptiness and delusion. There was a little boy who never forgot to make a profound salaam for all benefits received, and another who could open his mouth wider and bellow more penetratingly than any other child of the same age I had ever met. They were all quite irresistibly appealing and they soon had me completely captivated by their charms.

There was to me however, as a young doctor freshly out from Britain, something about these children that was disturbing. Their play, on the whole, was unimaginative. They tended too to be rather backward in development and to talk late. Why was this, I asked myself? They were receiving every care. Their diet was liberal and well balanced. They were well housed in surroundings that were both attractive and hygienic. They were provided with play-things, and early had the help and interest of nursery school. Most important of all it was obvious that they were very much loved. As I pondered this it seemed to me possible that the retarded development might be due to their living together in groups of approximately the same age. They lacked the stimulus to compete and to learn by imitation that life with children of mixed ages normally affords.

I took an early opportunity of telling Amma what I felt about this situation. She assured me that I was by no means the first to observe and comment on the disadvantage of rearing children in limited age-groups and of moving them frequently from the care of one person to another. However there were problems. Taking her illustrations from within the Family as it then existed she showed me a few of the difficulties which a change of method would entail. It needs a person of strong character and special ability to take complete charge of a family of children of mixed ages and to see them through all their vicissitudes from babyhood to adult life. It seemed that there were simply not enough such people available. Moreover besides a shortage of suitable personnel there were big administrative problems involved. Yet, characteristically, Amma observed that the mere fact that change would be difficult did not mean that it could not or should not be effected. She encouraged me to try to find a way round the problem.

These pages will show that a solution was eventually found and a change made. The credit, I should hasten to add, does not belong to me.

About six weeks after my arrival in Dohnavur, Dr. Christian Rogan left for furlough. For many years she had been responsible for the women's side of the hospital work as well as for the medical care of the women and children of the Family. When she left I took over the latter task from her at once. This gave me the opportunity to get to know people of all ages throughout the big community and to learn something of its life at first hand. Within the first year I met and came to know a representative cross-section of the more than eight hundred who comprised the Dohnavur Family of those days. It was like entering into the life of a small village, with its schools and hospital, gardens, farms and workshops, and with all its varied inhabitants and their different occupations and interests. The complexity of the task of providing for the spiritual and material, intellectual and physical needs of such a Family became devastatingly clear.

My own special interest was the hospital with its work for the people of the surrounding countryside. Whenever opportunity offered I took my cycle and rode out past the Babies' Place and the large pleasant houses where the little boys lived, and on over the bridge and down a long road where flame trees flaunted their brilliance against the blue background of the mountains. At the end of that road is the hospital. There I was quickly introduced to another aspect of the work in which I was to have some share.

4

Outreach

Squatting in the centre of the room the old lady was completely absorbed and did not notice our coming. With one foot steadying the flat stand of polished wood from which projected the graceful curve of a keen-bladed knife, she was busy cutting up vegetables. They were scattered round her on the red-tiled floor, little red onions and purple and green brinjals and others to which I could not put a name. A baby was crawling under the bed, while another small child played in a corner. On the bed itself a younger woman was sitting cross-legged, surveying the scene. She had taken the hospital sheet off the bed and was wearing it as a sari. She looked friendly, and I was about to practise my Tamil on her when a sharp, pungent smell hit me, catching my breath. I was suddenly overwhelmed with a violent fit of coughing and forced, with streaming eyes, to beat a hasty retreat. Whatever was that, I asked, that made me cough so uncontrollably? The people in the next room, I was told, were seasoning their curry with fried chillies.

Such scenes no longer surprise me, but when I first arrived I had not expected things to be quite like that in the private wards for paying patients.

The Place of Heavenly Healing (*Parama Suha Salai*), as the hospital is called, had been opened in 1936 under Dr. Murray Webb Peploe's leadership. The wards were designed in a way that made them acceptable to people of all religions, including the very strict upper-caste Hindus. There were facilities for the sick to have their families with them all the time and for each family to cook its meals in private according to its own traditions of ceremonial purity. This arrangement deliberately sacrificed medical convenience to evangelistic opportunity. Because their feelings were considered and their customs respected, and perhaps also because the service they were given was motivated by love rather than gain, people from the countryside around flocked to the hospital in ever-increasing numbers. By 1946 many thousands of Hindus and Muslims were attending the out-patient department, while hundreds were admitted to the wards each year.

Murray was an inspiring leader whose burning desire to commend his Lord to all and sundry overflowed into everything that he did or said. Following his example it seemed the right and natural thing for all members of staff to take their part in the evangelistic work. Many of them did their best to use the opportunities afforded by their work to tell their patients about the One who could meet all their deepest needs.

European missionary staff were in charge of each department. They were also responsible for training members of the Family (from which all workers were drawn) as nurses, dispensers and technicians, and also as helpers in the countless humdrum tasks which are so necessary to the efficient running of a hospital.

Amma told me again and again that the hospital was the Family's first mission field. She thought of it, not as a platform for preachers, but rather as a place where the love of Christ could be demonstrated in action, and thereafter explained in simple terms to those whose hearts were thereby opened to hear. I soon saw enough to realise that in the hospital people were in fact being won for Christ by this means.

Just after Christmas 1946 I was introduced to an important annual event, the Meetings of Vision. Even to my inexperienced eyes it was a moving sight to see the company, several hundred strong and drawn from many different castes, that assembled in our Gospel Hall for those meetings. The hospital wards had been partially vacated and converted into a conference centre. Invitations had been sent to people contacted through the medical work or through other evangelistic efforts, and the response was both surprising and encouraging. People cheerfully put up with simple accommodation and the barest hospitality in order to hear the Bible expounded and the Gospel explained. Year by year God has greatly blessed these Meetings which are still an annual event.

In 1945 a big move forward had been made in child evangelism, and by the end of 1946 this branch of the work was in a very flourishing state. Barbara Butler (later to become Mrs. Trehane) who was working among our own schoolgirls and teaching in the school, organised about sixty of them into three teams. These girls, with her help, ran two weekly meetings for Hindu children, including also boys up to the age of eleven. In addition the children of seven different villages were visited regularly in their own homes, while yet another meeting, attended by about eighty children, was held in a slightly more distant and very poor village. On Sundays there was a regular children's service. At a little later date a meeting was begun also in Dohnavur village just at our doors for nominally Christian girls. Early in 1947 David Aruldasan, at the request of the village Pastor, began too a similar meeting there for older boys.

Some, but not all, of these meetings have been continued until the time of writing. Through the years many children have been contacted, and as a result some have come to know the Lord Jesus as their personal Saviour and have shown evidence of their growth in Him.

Amma was always anxious to recruit new missionaries like myself to active, militant evangelism as soon as possible. "You must learn to *think* Tamil," was her repeated injunction to me, as she spoke of the evangelistic outreach of the hospital and of the Family in general. "You must know the people. You must know the way they think if you are ever going to get the Gospel across to them."

She did her best to hasten the process of learning by calling me almost every day to teach me a Tamil proverb (that most useful device for clinching an argument, or for turning a moment of tension into an occasion for laughter), or to acquaint me with some aspect of local custom or other helpful piece of background knowledge. Before long she decreed that I must start going out to villages "to teach", and so I was introduced to the Family's methods of village evangelism.

With an older Indian companion, chosen for her ability to pick up the bricks dropped by the new missionary, I would set out in the early evening across the brilliant green rice fields. Alas, I had no eyes for the stately white egrets standing lost in contemplation at the edge of the fields or wading with delicately lifted feet through the mud in search of frogs. Even the deep blue shadows in the folds of the mountains, or the bright saris of the women weeding the sunlit paddy left me unmoved. I was entirely pre-occupied with the Bible story I had laboriously learned by heart and must so soon tell to the object of our visitation. I went on muttering it miserably to myself as we walked, wondering whatever good could possibly come from my feeble efforts.

Arrived in the village however, I found much to distract, and was conscious of being on test and closely observed. It was better, one judged, to avoid head-on encounters with homeward-bound cows or buffaloes. All the scruffy dogs in the neighbourhood tended to come yapping round and must be tactfully negotiated. Rudely shouting or giggling children had to be smiled upon or ignored as the occasion seemed to demand. There were watchful eyes everywhere, appraising, disapproving, curious, or occasionally frankly welcoming. Women with large brass vessels on their hips would pause for a moment to speak to us before continuing on their way. Around the village well there was always a gossiping crowd of women, bathing themselves and their children, washing their clothes, or busy drawing water to take home for all household purposes.

There was one village where a high caste woman was always ready to welcome us, chiefly because she was grateful for help received in the hospital. Her ten-year-old daughter would usually see us coming and run to warn her mother to spread a mat for us on the verandah. Week after week, while the four- or five-year-old boy rampaged about, and the latest baby crawled around or howled for attention, mother and daughter would listen to our message. It was with almost incredulous joy that my companion and I realised eventually that our friend had experienced the miracle of the new birth. The Holy Spirit had worked to the glory of the Saviour through a weak and foolish instrument!

In other houses it was quite usual for the initial welcome to be mainly due to curiosity. Once I had been well inspected, and important points concerning my home and family, my customs with regard to food and bathing, or the price of my sari, had been cleared up, ill-concealed yawns would proclaim complete lack of interest in anything else we had to say.

Early in 1947 I gained further insight into the Family's potential outreach, and had the opportunity of learning more about village life at close quarters. With Indian companions I was sent to live in the small temple town to which reference has already been made. Our house was in the shepherd quarter, and we shared a courtyard with a widow woman and her mentally deranged daughter, a cow and a calf. At night we would hear the poor young woman's hopeless cries as, wailing and beating her head against the wall, she fruitlessly searched for her dead baby and her lost husband. The cow would stamp and low in mournful sympathy, making our sleep fitful. Very early in the morning the new day would be heralded by the sound of splashing water and sweeping as women tidied their houses and swept the adjacent street. This done the majority decorated the threshold of their homes with an intricate pattern traced in chalk-powder on the ground. With this adornment good housewives hoped to invoke the blessing of the goddess Lakshmi as she passed on her way at dawn.

While my companions set forward the mysteries of Indian cooking I sometimes took my morning meal up on to the roof so as to enjoy the luxury of solitude for a few moments before the business of the day really began. Coconut palms in the next garden carried on a friendly whispered conversation in the early morning breeze. The talk of women, the shouts of children and the odd noises made by the drivers of rumbling bullock carts drifted up from the street below and made a fitting background for my seclusion. But after only two or three days of this happy arrangement my quiet was rudely interrupted by the arrival of a troop of fierce monkeys which had discovered my presence and at once taken a fancy to my simple meal. I beat a pre-cipitate and undignified retreat, narrowly escaping the loss of my entire breakfast! The monkeys were a nuisance to everyone, but since they are regarded as sacred, nothing could be done to protect people's property, or even children, against their attacks.

The little town gave the impression that its way of life had continued unchanged for hundreds of years. No rumour of the swift developments of this twentieth century had penetrated there. For me much that I saw shed a vivid light on familiar Bible allusions—women grinding their grain between heavy mill-stones, winnowing fans in daily use, oxen treading the corn, oil-lamps as the only source of light at night, deep wells from which every drop of water must be laboriously drawn by hand. All this and much more was fascinating and picturesque, but how un-economic and extravagant of time and energy for the people who had to live this way! The agricultural resources of the countryside around were only partially developed because of lack of water. There was no electric current available for light or for power, and no other form of mechanisation had yet been introduced to save labour. Communications were still poor. There may have been two or three buses on the high road through the town in the course of twenty-four hours, but not more, and the roads were appalling. The advent of a car was a signal for a crowd to collect.

We visited poor little houses of mud and thatch on the out-skirts of the town and in near villages. There children swarmed in conditions of terrible overcrowding and dire poverty. The sight of some undernourished child covered in sores and constantly brushing away the flies from sticky infected eyes would some-times prompt me to offer medical advice. The people looked at me strangely and gave me polite and evasive answers. In Tamil too rapid for me to follow they told my companion that if they wanted medical help they would come to the other doctor. They trusted her because she understood their language.

We generally set out for our round of visiting laden with books and tracts for sale to anyone interested. At that time we were producing a steady flow of original literature in the Tamil book department whose programme was inspired and guided by Godfrey Webb Peploe in conjunction with some of the Indian brothers with literary gifts. Twenty-seven new books and booklets were produced during my first year in Dohnavur, and the book-room issued these and other publications to distributors in Tamil-nad at the rate of many thousands every week. In the villages near Dohnavur, however, we seldom found a woman who could read and who wanted to buy. Schoolboys were our best customers. It was rare at any level of society to find girls who were continuing with their education after the age of ten or eleven, and if all learning is abandoned at so early a stage, it is easy to lapse back into near-illiteracy. Most adolescent girls were kept in strict seclusion and, according to traditional custom, for-bidden to see any man except their own father and brothers until the day of their marriage. This was, of course, arranged for them by their parents and they themselves had no say at all in it.

In many houses we were welcome. The stories we told provided a diversion in the monotony of the lives of the women and girls. Often in the evening when most of their work was finished a group of them would listen with real interest. Then suddenly one of them would excuse herself. Soon she would be absorbed in the rite of lamp-lighting. First she would hang a delicate garland of pale oleander flowers over the tall brass lamp-stand, and then light the tiny floating wick and perform her evening *puja* before the pictures of the gods which adorn the walls of nearly every orthodox Hindu house. Dawn and dusk alike were marked by acts of devotion, and religion was part of the fabric of life.

Occasionally we were courteously entertained on the verandah of a Brahman house under the very shadow of the ancient temple walls. These folk did not defile their houses by inviting us inside, and their courtesy was generally a mark of gratitude for help received in the hospital. As a rule they had no time or inclination to listen to our message. They, almost more than anyone else, seemed bound by age-long custom and tradition.

Nevertheless the wind of change was beginning to blow ever so softly. Even in that very town a progressive Brahman family had a daughter in a medical college, and a son studying modern agricultural methods in the United States.

Now and again gangs of youths would follow us shouting "White dog, get out". Older folk sometimes went out of their way to assure me that the young were very foolish and should not be heeded. All the same, change was on the way; indeed it was on the very threshold.

5

Change

"*Jai Hind! Jai Hind!*" Suddenly one evening the unfamiliar slogan rang out, echoing and re-echoing about our boundary walls. The words mean "Victory to Hindustan" and had become the battle cry of Indian nationals seeking, very understandably, their country's independence of foreign rule. In the present context however they had little political significance and were merely being bawled by a group of malcontents from among our otherwise friendly village neighbours. These had lodged a petition against us alleging that we had unlawfully closed a public road. Lacking any vestige of legal grounds for their complaint, they sought for some months to bolster it by stirring up local agitation of various kinds.

On one such occasion a gang of young men, all set to take the law into their own hands and break through our gates, gathered in the street outside with much shouting and commotion. Suddenly the gates were thrown open from within and they were stunned into apprehensive silence to find themselves looking up at the tall, well-known figure of the District Judge. His remarks were brief and to the point. The gang quietly melted away and the gates remained intact. The Judge, who had known nothing of our troubles, had unexpectedly come over on a friendly visit. We could not help feeling however that its date must have been planned in heaven.

Another group of some fifty youths hatched a plan of violence and were preparing to carry it out when a woman warned them that they were running into trouble. She had, she said, irrefutable evidence that we were specially protected by a very powerful God "who actually hears and answers their prayers". They abandoned their plan. We have again and again had cause to be grateful that what she said is completely true.

In this year of 1947 there were labour troubles too in the district. The big irrigation lake or reservoir from which our rice-land is watered needed desilting. With no bull-dozers on hand this was a tremendous task, and the local labour force was out on a Communist-instigated strike. Nothing daunted, the men and boys of our own Family undertook the work themselves. They completed it during April and May, the hot-weather holiday, in a spirit of gay camaraderie which made a picnic of what could easily have been a difficult situation.

Independence Day, August 15th 1947, passed off quietly enough here. Amid varied feelings the novel flag with its wheel of Asoka on a background of saffron, white and green was run up for the occasion on the tall flag-staff in the playing field. It was a new day in India's long history. A familiar order had passed and the nation moved expectantly into a future still unknown.

The first news was stark tragedy. The newspapers told of riots and massacres in the north, Muslims against Hindus, Sikhs against Muslims. Hundreds of thousands were dying in the conflict, and fifteen million innocent folk had been uprooted to become refugees. But here in the predominantly Hindu south these terrible consequences of Partition seemed mercifully remote, and made little direct impact on the life of the villages even where there were vulnerable Muslim minorities. And in due course the new Government got the measure of things, and over-all quiet was restored.

India's real quarrel had been with the concept of foreign rule and domination. Her responsible leaders, mature statesmen like Mahatma Gandhi and Jawaharlal Nehru, were not unfriendly to the British as people, nor even to Britain as a nation once she was prepared to accord to India the right to self-government. The very minor troubles that we ourselves experienced were no true reflection of national policy. Yet there were not lacking dismal prophets, both in India and abroad, who declared that within five years of Independence all British nationals would undoubtedly receive summary notice to quit.

In my own moments of depression there returned to mind with nagging persistence the warnings of those who a year or so earlier had sought to discourage me from leaving England. Were they right? Had it been a mistake to come? Still new to the work, and frustrated by the handicaps of inexperience and inadequate Tamil, I felt myself to be even now only a passenger. Was there to be, as they had gloomily forecast, an ignominious return to the home country before I had had time to accomplish anything at all for God in the work to which He had sent me? How possible it is to let oneself be dominated by thoughts such as these, and thus to become engulfed in a morass of self-pity!

Happily it is equally possible to know the exhilaration of treading the path of God's choice with Him, confident that, even when human wisdom suggests there is no future in such a course, experience will yet prove Him an utterly trustworthy Guide.

Although I had not been here long enough to do anything very constructive for the Family, there had been time to become deeply involved in its life and fortunes. It was easy to see how important, nay, how urgent it was to plan for the maintenance and security of the work in the event of Europeans being withdrawn at short notice. My own worries dwindled into insignificance before the magnitude of this task. The future of the missionaries, myself included, seemed far less precarious than that of all the children and young folk, and older ones too, who might be left to fend for themselves in a non-Christian and unsympathetic environment. Unavoidably they had till now been very dependent on the foreign members of the Fellowship. What might be their future if robbed of this protection and help? It was evident that they themselves were beginning anxiously to ask this question.

A sense of insecurity, always the bane of young people deprived of normal family life and parental care, began here and there to manifest itself. Insidiously a mood of unease and apprehension spread through the Family, and was further fanned by rumours and speculative talk, over and above the authentic news of changes that were abroad everywhere. It was a situation that might easily explode into something approaching panic.

But to all who thus looked into the future with misgivings or worse, there remained one great comfort and reassurance. In the gracious provision of God their beloved Amma was still present with them in Dohnavur.

True, she was by now ageing and invalid, unable any longer to be to them either personally or administratively the tower of strength she had proved in years past. Yet her spiritual gifts and vision shone out undimmed. She had led them through great experiences; could she not lead them still?

Amma herself had several times urged that someone else should be appointed as official leader of the work her labours had brought into being. The Family however would not hear of this. She was not just their leader; was she not their mother? and you could not alter that! In any and every crisis young and old alike had been accustomed to turn to her for understanding sympathy, comfort and wise counsel. How could anyone ever take her place?

Of course in practice the administrative burden was more widely shared, and God had given to the work men and women of spiritual stature for the task. It is true that one of these, Murray Webb Peploe, had already been compelled for family reasons to leave for England early in 1947, but his gifted brother Godfrey remained as the wholly acceptable leader of the boys' work and loved *Annachie* (elder brother) to the entire Family. On the girls' side too Dr. May Powell, who for years had acted as Amma's deputy in practical matters, had so earned the trust of the women workers as to become a real strength to the Family during this phase of uncertainty. And these two were supported by a loyal band of experienced men and women from several lands of Europe and the Commonwealth, working alongside the Indian women and senior men whom Amma herself had trained. Yet the weight of responsibility fell largely upon the missionary team— and this in a day when the role of foreign administrators seemed growingly anachronous. Small wonder therefore if some in the Family felt restive and unsettled.

Towards the end of 1947 two days were set apart for quiet waiting upon the Lord in prayer. We are accustomed to give one day to prayer each month, but this was something extra, planned to meet a deeply felt need. In writing of it Amma drew from Scripture words that she felt defined the object of those days. Quoting from Ezra 8 : 21: "I proclaimed a fast there by the river Ahava, that we might *lower* ourselves before God to seek of him a right way for us, and for our little ones, and for all our substance," she wrote: "There was need for this sort of prayer. In various ways the powers of evil were threatening the work and injuring it. Some problems were insoluble. We needed light."

God is ever near to those who call upon Him. He met us during those days, and, as we needed it, light began to be given upon the path—yet not without a further severe shaking, both local and India-wide. At the end of January 1948 all India was profoundly shocked by the assassination of Mahatma Gandhi at the hand of a religious fanatic. Such an outrage could only throw a dark shadow of fear and foreboding over the newly established Republic. Indians everywhere went into deep mourning for the beloved father of the nation. Uneasy dread of an unstable future seemed more than ever justified.

That summer in our small world a different blow fell. One evening Amma slipped in her room, fell heavily and was gravely injured. Some of us were called urgently to her help. There she lay, shocked and ill on the floor. A splint of some kind was essential to help lift her to her bed. In a moment of inspiration someone took from the wall a long, rough-carved plank on which had been painted the words "Good . . . Acceptable . . . Perfect", and with its help the painful, delicate task was skilfully completed.

It was a fitting plank for faith to rest upon! Although the remaining two and a half years of Amma's life held their fill of pain as her weakness increased, yet to the end of her days she rested unmoved in that "good and acceptable and perfect will of God".

In the event, Amma's retirement from effective leadership was compelled by this accident. Gradually but irrevocably the Family came to accept the fact, and to realise that the moment of her fall had effected the greatest change they had so far experienced.

6

Leadership

The world of India into which our little children would grow up was already a very different place from that in which their elders had lived until now. By the first months of 1949 almost all secular posts of political and administrative importance had passed into the hands of nationals. It was only natural that within the Christian Church and its mission institutions, ours among them, the parallel need for national leadership should be urgently felt.

There is no doubt that missionary work in India had for years been influenced by what its critics would now call the "imperialistic outlook". Everywhere Christian enterprise was under foreign direction and largely financed by foreign funds. Many missionaries had unconsciously adopted towards their Indian fellow workers a benignly paternal attitude, ill-fitted to the training of robust independent Christians able to manage their own affairs with God alone for Guide and Supplier of their needs.

In some respects Amma's vision for the future of the work she was building up was ahead of her times. She had always thought in terms of equal co-operation between Indian and European workers. Comradeship was the word she used to describe the conception. As early as 1927 she had named her friend and colleague Arulai Tara as the one she considered most suited for the future leadership of the enterprise.* But it was not to be. God had other thoughts, and He took Arulai to be with Himself at a comparatively early age.

After this disappointment it sometimes seemed that, where the rest of the Family were concerned, Amma found it hard to believe her beloved children had really grown up. Consequently she never, perhaps, fully realised that they had reached a stage when they should be assigned exactly the same tasks and responsibilities as the European missionaries, and that exactly the same standards could be expected of them in fulfilling those tasks. It was thus painfully true that at this critical stage in the work there were few if any of the Indian Family with the experience and training necessary for leadership in a larger context.

Readers will doubtless realise that the work at Dohnavur is locally autonomous, and not guided in any way from any overseas headquarters. It was for us here, and us alone, to find God's way for us through this time of crisis and transition.

The Council Minutes of January 1949 record the formal nomination and election of Godfrey Webb Peploe as co-leader of the Fellowship. Amma had been completely bed-ridden for rather more than six months, and was quite unable any longer to fulfil the heavy programme of interviews and writing which had filled her days up to the time of her accident. Although many in the Family were still earnestly praying and hoping for her miraculous restoration to health, they were at last beginning to realise that it was now essential that someone be fully authorised to make

* See Frank Houghton, *Amy Carmichael of Dohnavur*, London, 1953, p. 356.

important decisions without her. They trusted Godfrey. They trusted May Powell too, who though not yet formally appointed as a co-leader, continued in many matters to deputise for Amma, and so in practice often had to take responsibilities that amounted to that. The work was too large for one alone.

In February, with the future still in view, seven more Indian men and women were nominated for membership of the Fellowship. This implied that in their hearts was a firm conviction, and one borne out by their lives, that God had called and separated them to the work in Dohnavur. It implied too that gifts of initiative, leadership, and the strength to carry responsibility were already apparent in them, and that these were matched by a humble spirit of service.

Such are the marks looked for in any who are invited to consider full membership of the Fellowship. There are of course many others in the Family who have not all these qualities, but who are nevertheless trusted colleagues and fellow-workers in a true sense. Of necessity any large work of this kind must have its inner circle of those who share with the leaders the burden of prayer and responsibility, and our Fellowship members constitute this inner circle. But at this time Europeans very far outnumbered Indians in its membership and the election of the seven new members was a step towards rectifying this imbalance.

Just five days after the meeting at which these new members had been nominated, God took Godfrey from us. He had been ill, but this outcome was completely unforeseen and his death came as a devastating shock to us all.

Our loving God is very courageous. Observers had often said that the work in Dohnavur was built up around Amma's personality and could not continue to exist without her. For her part she had always maintained that God was its unseen and all-sufficient Leader, and that the work that had been built upon Him and for His glory alone depended in no way on its human founder. Now He was putting this to the proof, hazarding His reputation as it were, by stripping us of our human supports, risking possible collapse and failure that must inevitably bring dishonour to His Name. He was shaking the foundations of our security to prove whether they were soundly laid in Himself. He was allowing the fire of testing to pass over us that we might prove that in that fire His presence with us was sufficient.

The news of Godfrey's death sent through all our hearts a pang of unspeakable grief. The shock of it left us numbed. Godfrey was gone—Godfrey the evangelist and Tamil scholar and gifted counsellor of men; Godfrey the naturalist and musician and athlete, the gentle elder brother and presumptive heir to the leadership. To the Family as a whole it was mystifying enough; to Amma herself it was both a very great personal loss—for she had loved him as a dear son—and a crushing blow to her hopes for the future.

It was never her way, however, to expend valuable time and energy in self-pity, so her first act was to send a brief note to us all urging courage and steadfastness. "This is a great trust," she wrote. "Our God trusts us to trust Him and to rejoice because our beloved Annachie has gone to the Father. Let us not disappoint God. Let us rise to this great trust."

When she had had time to collect her thoughts a little more, she wrote a longer letter. In it she said: "Perhaps we shall never again have such a chance to glorify our God as we have now. Don't let us lose this chance to show His great enemy and all the unseen watchers that we do indeed trust our Father, and that nothing, not even this sore parting, can for a moment shake our confidence in Him."

The Family rallied to this challenge with strength and courage, and Godfrey's funeral was turned into an opportunity for witness to the many who came from the surrounding countryside. In the hospital, where the staff are closely observed by the patients, work went quietly on in a way that must have been pleasing to our Lord, and that made some observers ask the reason for the hope that is ours.

During the night of Godfrey's death Amma wrote a little note to John Risk, Godfrey's lieutenant and understudy. She assured him of her prayers, and declared her belief that he was the one of God's choice for the vacant position of co-leader. In due course he was formally elected to that office. A considerably younger man, he had nevertheless served long in Dohnavur and knew and understood the Family very well. But he had of course never thought of himself in terms of leadership. His was a somewhat intense nature, and the suddenly imposed task must have come upon him as a specially heavy burden. However he was not one to shirk anything that he knew to be his duty, and he took it up unhesitatingly and unselfishly for love of his Lord.

As the months passed Amma's health steadily deteriorated until it became obvious, even to the most tenaciously optimistic, that she could not be with us much longer. There was no one person left now who was conversant as she had been with the background and intimate details of everyone's personal history. On the other hand the Family had clearly outstepped the bounds of such intimate knowledge on the part of any one person; for the work had grown in a way that she had never foreseen, and in her last years she can scarcely have realised the full implications of its vastly increased numbers. It had become clear that leadership could no longer be a one-man assignment. Henceforth it must be a shared responsibility.

For some weeks early in 1950 the members of the Fellowship gave extra time each day to meet and pray together for God's guidance in this matter so important to the future of the work.

Eventually we were all agreed that the leadership should be entrusted to a small group whom God would choose. Theirs would be the task of overall executive responsibility. They would deal too with the many daily problems that crop up in a community such as ours and demand immediate action. In the out-working, their burden is a heavy one and they find it necessary to meet almost every day. They count it their first responsibility to bring all our affairs to God in prayer, and to seek to discover His will concerning each detail.

John Risk as co-leader, and May Powell who was called to a parallel role at about this time, became *ex officio* members of the group as first constituted. They were joined by Norman Burns, Margaret Wilkinson, and Rajappan, eldest son of the Mimosa who gives her name to one of Amma's earliest writings.*

There thus emerged the following pattern of concentric circles of responsibility: i, two Co-leaders; ii, a "Leadership Group" of five; iii, the Council; and iv, the Fellowship.

The Council was next enlarged to be more representative of the whole Family than hitherto, and considerably more business was assigned to it. Until 1947 it had been an entirely missionary body which met at rare intervals. Now two Indian members were appointed to it and soon a third. It began to meet regularly twice each month as an administrative and advisory body on matters of principle and major policy. It is, as well, a training ground for potential future leaders.

Any decision involving a change of policy or the formulation of a new principle is brought first to the Council and eventually to the whole Fellowship. We ask the Lord to bring us to unanimity at every stage before any really major decision is implemented, and do not act until we are all sure He is unmistakably leading us to do so. Our daily Fellowship prayer meetings are an immensely

* Amy Carmichael, *Mimosa, who was charmed*, Madras, S.P.C.K., 1925.

important factor contributing to this unity and unanimity. As together we bring to God in united intercession different aspects of our many-sided work, we do so in the conviction that it is in fact He who is our true Leader. It is He who in all essentials must give us the lead.

7

The Square

Meenila and her friends were still young enough to be quite
unaware of the events which were giving their elders so much
food for thought. Nevertheless change had dogged their footsteps
also.

At the age of two Meenila had been moved to "The Square".
Here, at that time, little girls between the ages of two and eight
lived in small family groups with their Accals. The Square derives
its name from the arrangement of a dozen cottage homes around
the four sides of an open grassy space where the children can play.
It is a pleasant place, with shady margosa trees and brightly
flowering shrubs of oleander and hibiscus and frangipani. Yellow-
blossomed creepers adorn the trellised verandahs beneath low-
pitched cottage roofs of interlocking Travancore tiles.

Meenila's new home was in one of these little cottages, clean
and attractive with its simple teak furniture and gleaming brass
vessels, and with a tiled floor that glowed a deep red from much
vigorous polishing. To it her new Accal, whose name was Anna-

mai, gave her a loving and joyous welcome. All the same it was a devastating experience, when night came, to lie down in these unfamiliar surroundings. Desolate she cried herself to sleep, missing, more than she knew, the well-loved Accal who had mothered her for as long as she could remember.

The fact, however, that another of the "Pearls" had moved with her, and was here now alongside her in the same room, did something to soften the blow of the move. The two of them shared their toys and played together during the day. The other six or seven children in the house were also about Meenila's age, and had all earlier been with her in "The Place of Babies", so she was not separated from her friends.

Gradually she settled down and became adjusted to her different circumstances and programme, and soon her happiness returned. She continued to go to nursery school as she had from the Bala Stala. She enjoyed this very much. Generally she was quick and intelligent and soon developed a marked manual dexterity. She was so proud of herself when she had managed to thread beads on a string in correctly alternating colours that at once she donned it as a garland; but when she could not make her material do what she wanted, she would lie on the floor and give vent to her frustration by kicking and yelling lustily. It would take her a long time to get over one of these bouts of temper. Sometimes, however, when things went wrong, she would relieve her feelings by pinching the child next to her. It was then of course unnecessary to do the screaming herself.

Meenila's Accal kept some white rabbits for the sake of the children. The child became passionately fond of these furry creatures. One night, having seen her family of children safely to bed, Annamai was doing a last tour of inspection with a lantern. Most of them were already sound asleep, but the small blue-sheeted mound that was Meenila writhed and wriggled mysteriously. Was something wrong with the child? Annamai lifted back the sheet. Meenila was anxiously grappling with a large white rabbit which she was bent on "looking after" for the night.

"Nothing can hurt it if I cuddle it," she assured her Accal.

Annamai was not so certain. She had visions of the poor creature suffocating slowly to death, and of Meenila's consequent grief and distress. She gently explained that bunny liked to run about at night, and eventually persuaded the tearful child to carry it to its hutch. Only after fervently hugging and kissing it could she bring herself to say goodnight and leave it.

Meenila had a strong will of her own and did not find it easy to obey; but she had too a very loving heart and could not bear it if things were wrong between herself and another. If, during the day, her temper or her disobedience had got her into trouble, she could not rest until she had said she was sorry and had been forgiven. From her earliest years she was an honest and truthful child. Even as a very small girl, if she knew that one of her friends had fallen to the temptation of helping herself to someone else's food or sweets, she would do her utmost to get the offender to confess what she had done. She knew she must not tell tales, but she hated to have anything dishonest concealed from her Accal.

Her ability to raise a laugh by her gift of mimicry made her popular with her contemporaries, and was the despair of her seniors. When she was still a very little girl and was out for an evening walk, the group met a lame man hobbling awkwardly along the road. All at once there was a howl of mirth from the children. Annamai easily spotted its source. The laugh had been raised by Meenila's lifelike caricature of the poor man's grotesque gait. She explained later to Meenila how much the man himself must have been suffering. Meenila had not thought of that and was horrified, and never again did

she make fun of the maimed or handicapped. But she
was by no means through with her mimicking.

It was about this time that Meenila had a severe illness, and
herself learned something about suffering from personal experience. Along with several other children with feverish colds, she
had been taken across the dry watercourse that lies outside the
western gates and up the long avenue of flame trees that leads to
the hospital, to be admitted to the section of wards in which our
own Family are cared for when they are ill. In an effort to limit
the spread of infection among the children we admit all cases of
fever to the wards in this way. Here in these quiet surroundings
with their distant glimpses of forest-clad mountain peaks, special
care can be given to young and old. Meenila's illness was initially
a mild one, and she was soon back home with her friends in the
Square again.

But just about three weeks later, flushed and in pain, she was
urgently re-admitted. This time it was clear that she was gravely
ill. She had in fact developed acute rheumatic fever. For some
days it was difficult to find any way of easing the pain which kept
returning to torment her afresh in bouts that made her scream out
with distress. It is never easy to see a child suffer, and Meenila's
agonised expression went straight to our hearts.

After a few miserable days the worst was over, and she began
to be her cheerful self again. For some of us however, acquainted
with the ways of the illness she had contracted, the anxiety was
by no means yet relieved. Every few days I carefully examined her
heart to try to assess the damage done to it by this devastatingly
severe attack. She rather enjoyed this. There are some pieces of
medical equipment which lend themselves to games with the
young, and the stethoscope is one. It has endless possibilities.
So our sessions were cheerful, even if my own heart was heavy
with forebodings. What future was there for a child with a

damaged heart? She made fair progress but her stay in hospital was necessarily prolonged. It was not until fully six months had passed that we thought her fit to rejoin her set. Only then could she begin to resume a more or less normal life.

8

Education

My night in the train had been definitely "third class". Now towards noon the house to which it had brought me was stuffy and airless, and I was feeling the heat. Slowly the waves of grateful slumber enveloped and overwhelmed me and I sank unresisting into luxurious oblivion. All at once a shattering noise recalled me abruptly to consciousness. Where was I? Whatever could be happening? I struggled to throw off the oppressive weight of interrupted sleep. Dragging myself to the open window I looked out.

So that was it! Down the centre of the sunbaked road, bouncing and clanging madly on their way, there rolled a long procession of empty metal oil-drums. Each great drum was pursued by a relentless coolie whose task it was to kick it clattering onward to its destination. What would they think of next!

Now I remembered. This was Trichy,* and the house I was in

* Tiruchirapalli, formerly Trichinopoly and thus "Trichy", is an important railway junction some two hundred miles to the north of us.

was the hostel from which nine of our teen-age girls were attending the big high school just down the road.

It had been fun to join them at their morning meal when I came off the train. They had fired questions at me non-stop because I had come straight from Dohnavur, and so was a potential source of precious home news. Perhaps we talked rather long, for suddenly, the meal over, the house was thrown into turmoil as these ebullient youngsters sped around doing their last minute chores. The snatches of conversation, yelps of dismay and groans of horror that reached me were all in Tamil, it is true, but they seemed to cover long familiar ground. "Who's got my pen?" "Hasn't *anyone* seen my homework book?" "Sittie, what's the time? Can't I just . . ." "*Aiyo!* This chapter was to be learnt for today. I'd quite forgotten!" Frantically they collected their scattered belongings, and some contrived a last minute session with a mirror to add those significant final touches to hair and sari that spelt style. Then at last they were all set to go. Cheerily they cascaded out of the house and down the street, as lively and colourful a group as one could wish to see anywhere.

Now another night in the train. To describe this one as third class would be sheer flattery. But eventually it was over, and I reached my goal in North Arcot District, namely, the Christian Medical College and Hospital at Vellore. Here I was once more on ground that stirred familiar memories. The vital, purposeful atmosphere of a large teaching hospital is always stimulating, and all the more so in this Eastern setting. The unusual cases that I spotted within the first hour or two would have been the envy of any equivalent western hospital, but the patients, as people, fascinated me even more. Waiting-rooms and corridors teemed with them. There were betrousered Punjabi women with delicate scarves worn back to front over their shoulders, Muslim wives peering secretively through the small meshed slit in their all-enveloping burkas, Sikh men in turbans and beards, and followers of the Prophet in their fezes. Many were in immaculate European-style tropical suits and so were harder to place. There were speakers of Tamil and Malayalam, of Telugu, Kannada and Hindi, and of many more unidentified languages. The highly qualified staff in their clean white coats were drawn from many nations of the world and were obviously dedicated, to a man, to this tremendous enterprise in the service of medical education. The young women students I encountered added intelligence to their good looks, and to my seeming, conditioned as I was to country folk, they appeared highly sophisticated.

I sought out and soon found Suseela who for years had been in charge of our own hospital dispensary in Dohnavur. Now she was studying pharmacy for a year at Vellore in order to obtain the State certificate which would give official sanction to the position she had held unofficially for so long. Her classmates were mostly boys and girls just out of high school, whereas she was over forty. Yet in spite of this she had clearly succeeded in establishing happy relations and had won her way in this cosmopolitan and progressive institution, so different from our small rural hospital.

At the end of the year she passed her examinations, coming easily first in her class, and returned to Dohnavur to resume her responsibilities there. But this is to anticipate.

Why were these members of the Dohnavur Family studying so far from home in this spring of 1950?

It had all started about a year earlier. For by the beginning of 1949 some of India's new aims and policies in the field of social service had begun to emerge. There was to be a revolutionary speed-up of primary education. A great drive towards universal literacy was promised. More higher education would be made available for more and more young people, girls included. Schools were to be strictly inspected and must be staffed only by teachers holding State-recognised certificates that qualified them for the grade of work upon which they were engaged.

This posed for us some problems. How was it going to affect our own extensive work and the status of our staff? What would be the repercussions for our children's future?

Until now they had all been educated entirely in our own schools in Dohnavur. There were some obvious advantages in this arrangement. The influences of home and school could be made complementary to each other, planned and directed towards the same ends. In their young and impressionable years the children were not confused by differing standards of Christian behaviour or conflicting views about the Bible. Our schools had been staffed by European missionaries holding appropriate academic qualifications, and by Indian men and women who had grown up in Dohnavur and been educated and trained by them. These Indian teachers had been selected not only for their professional skill but even more for their spiritual calibre. The whole team, Indian and missionary, were one in seeking not merely to give the children a good formal education but also to train them up to know and serve the Lord. But alas, these Indian teachers held no certificates which the new Government would recognise as valid.

We had to ask ourselves therefore how these young men and women would fare should the State introduce compulsory inspection of all schools? Suppose, too, that institutions felt to be incorrectly staffed were to be summarily closed? The prospect was quite alarming.

One day early in 1949, with their minds full of questions such as these, May Powell and Margaret Wilkinson went to see Amma. She was bedridden, but her room was always gay with flowers and her table piled with books. Often there was a tame forest song-bird loose in her room or a golden cocker spaniel companionably asleep at her feet. Alpine and Himalayan paintings adorned the walls, and the place somehow conveyed the wide interests and sympathies of its occupant.

The immediate purpose of this visit was to ask Amma's blessing on the formation of a Guide Company in Dohnavur. Community life imposed a semblance of compulsion, or at least conformity, upon so many of the Family's activities. Margaret, who wanted to launch the project, saw in this completely voluntary organisation fresh scope for developing character and initiative in those who, it was hoped, would join.

Amma was comparatively well that day, and her mind seemed as clear and alert as it used to be when she was much younger. The soundness of Margaret's proposal appealed to her.

Noticing this May took the opportunity to talk to her about the changes taking place in India, and their likely repercussions on our work, and particularly on the education of our children. She mentioned too the Government's concern with the training of nurses, dispensers, laboratory technicians and other ancillary medical workers. How would our schools and our hospital stand in official esteem if their only certificated staff were foreigners?

It seemed essential to keep our children at home at least for the primary stage of their education, and also to preserve our freedom to run the hospital along lines that we felt had been shown us by God Himself. In order to do this, should we not consider sending some of our young people to Government-recognised schools and places of training? With properly qualified nationals in key positions, were we not more likely to be free to continue the most vital aspects of our work unhindered?

Amma closely followed May's reasoning, grasping the main issue with her old astuteness. She saw with them that the time had indeed come to avail ourselves of the expanding facilities beyond our walls so that our young people might secure the qualifications demanded for the correct staffing of our own schools and hospital. She even gave Margaret the name of the headmistress of a large girl's high school in Trichy who she thought might be able to help and advise us. She urged her to start enquiries at once, and to begin to make tentative plans.

In point of fact a small group of schoolboys had already been attending the C.M.S. Middle School at our gates for almost a year. The decision to send them there had, at the time it was taken, been a temporary measure and not a matter of policy. In retrospect, however, it seemed that the step had been directed by God in answer to our prayer for light in the Quiet Days of December 1947. Though unpremeditated it proved to be the first move towards a whole new policy into which stage by stage, He in fact planned to lead us.

In due course the first group of carefully chosen schoolgirls set out on the great new adventure of life in a big city and education in a large high school. Barbara Butler went with them to Trichy to run a hostel from which they could attend school as day-scholars. They had everything to learn about life in the outside world, and since they were a spirited group with plenty of original ideas of their own, there was never a dull moment in their first year away. Next year a somewhat larger group joined them at the same school.*

In the meanwhile the boys attended a high school near home. But buses were inconvenient and a lot of time was wasted on the long walk there and back. So next year they too went to a more distant school, and, at the suggestion of the headmaster, one of their own *Annachies*† went with them to run for them a boarding hostel. This man, Devapiriam, took the opportunity while there

* Their adventures have been recorded by Barbara Trehane (née Butler) in *The Timothys*, London, Lutterworth, 1958.

† *Annachie*, "elder brother" in Tamil (corresponding to *accal*, "elder sister") is an affectionate title that can be given to any older man, and is used in our Family for both Indians and Europeans.

to study for matriculation, which he sat and passed. Later he
went on to a teacher training college and obtained a Secondary
Grade Teachers' certificate. Married and with a family, he already
had years of teaching experience behind him, so this course of
study represented real sacrifice and self-discipline on his part.

But Devapiriam had clearly understood the need, and he
returned at length to Dohnavur to become Headmaster of the
Boys' School. Today he is a valued member of the Fellowship and
of the Council, with a big contribution to make to our life and
work.

On the women's side too there were those who recognised the
demands of the new situation, and who were prepared to pay the
price of study, often late in life and in their spare time, for public
examinations. Several, having passed the qualifying examinations
in general education, went on to teacher training colleges. Those
who went through with this arduous self-preparation are still
the backbone of the girls' and women's work here in Dohnavur,
and carry their share of administration as Fellowship members.

Happily we were able also to send some of our hospital staff-
workers for training in nursing and in some of the ancillary
medical services, without in their case the need for a preliminary
examination in general education. Several so trained at that time
are also back with us now in positions of trust and responsibility.

As set forth here, the need for such a change of policy seems
fairly obvious, and the steps taken may sound easy. At the time
it seemed otherwise. In the hospital, for example, the amount of
work coming to us had greatly increased and the country folk
needed our help acutely. In spite of this God led us to send some
of our most reliable senior workers, men and women, away to
other institutions for training. On certain of the less stable juniors
the effect of this step seemed disastrous. They could not wait
their turn. They too must get away into the wider and more

exciting life of the cities. Several of them lost their sense of vocation, and left us to seek their fortunes elsewhere. We thus found ourselves so short of staff that for a time we were obliged with great reluctance to close the men's side of the hospital completely. This most painful step seemed to us like deliberately closing a door of opportunity. We set ourselves to pray for more helpers, and hoped that this closure would indeed be a temporary measure only.

Many years have passed now, and we have no cause to regret the decision which led on to radical changes in our whole educational policy. Temporary loss and difficulty were to lead on to permanent gain. Amma herself played a large part in this initial decision, but she was never again able to share in the formulation of new plans and new advances.

9

The End of an Era

Early on the morning of January 18th 1951 the bells of the House of Prayer began to chime. The tune was that of one of Amma's own songs:

> One thing have I desired, my God, of Thee,
> That will I seek, Thine house be home to me.
>
> I would not breathe an alien, other air,
> I would be with Thee, O Thou fairest Fair.
>
> For I would see the beauty of my Lord,
> And hear Him speak, who is my heart's Adored.

Annamai heard and understood the message of those bells. For the past two days Amma had lain unconscious while her Family had come and gone, saying their last goodbyes. Early that morning before it was light, word had been passed round that she was sinking fast, and that it would not be long now before her heart's desire would be fulfilled and she would be in the presence of the One who was everything to her.

Annamai continued her routine tasks for the children, but when they had all had their morning meal she could contain herself no longer and went into her little private room to hide from them her tears.

The bells went on and on, and they carried a message of comfort:

> O Love of loves, and can such wonder dwell
> In Thy great Name of names, Immanuel?
> Thou with Thy child, Thy child at home with Thee,
> O Lord my God, I love, I worship Thee.

In spite of the comfort of the words she knew so well, Annamai's tears continued to flow. Meenila crept into the room.

"Why are you crying?" she asked in great concern.

"Amma has left us, and gone to be with the Lord Jesus," explained her Accal.

"Then why are you crying?" asked Meenila, genuinely puzzled. "I am so glad that Amma has no more pain." She wiped away her Accal's tears, and then ran back to the other children clapping her hands. "Amma has no more pain and she is so happy with the Lord Jesus," she announced.

. . .

Piety and devotion are qualities which command respect in this land. Amma's single-hearted allegiance to the Lord whom she worshipped, and her sincere love of the people whom she served, had earned her the awed veneration of the countryside in which she had lived for so long. A group of her old servants carried her to the village church where she lay surrounded with flowers while Christians and Hindus came to pay their last respects. Many were old enough to recall earlier days; they remembered the long nights she had spent in their homes during epidemics of cholera, doing all she knew to help them and with never a thought for herself.

She had had no modern drugs, no trained nurse or doctor, but many owed to her their lives. The Christians had not forgotten her powerful appeals to them to have done with worldly compromise, and to yield full obedience to the Lord whose name they bore. Yes they remembered, but how few had been prepared to pay the price she had asked of unreserved committal to their God!

Every effort was made to buy up the opportunity of that day. Our boys and men, led by John Risk, went to the village church to share the people's sorrow, and while the crowds streamed in and out they sang every triumphant song they knew about Heaven and the Lord's ultimate victory over death and the dark powers. Every member of the congregation received a previously prepared card on which were printed verses telling of eternal life and the way of salvation. The Right Rev. George Selwyn, Bishop in Tirunelveli, one of Amma's oldest friends in India, arrived in time to lead the funeral service in the church.

Later we had our own private service of thanksgiving and committal in the House of Prayer and in the garden where she was laid to rest. The Family were valiant in their determination to rejoice in the joy of the one they had loved so well, and to remember all she had always taught them about courage and faith. We saw the enabling grace of God in many of them that day and in the days that followed.

With the going of our beloved Amma an era had ended; but He who is her Lord and ours did not leave us. She had proved His faithfulness through fifty-five years of unbroken service in India. In the new and varied experiences ahead of us we ourselves were to prove that faithfulness over and over again.

10

God Is Faithful

In 1951, our first year without Amma, our minds were occupied with new anxieties and new plans for the future. We were caught up willy nilly in the eager race for advance and improvement in the progressive new Republic of India. The vital question was: Were we receiving fresh inspiration from God Himself for our multitudinous activities? Or were we trading on experiences of the past? Amma had been characterised by a fervent love for her Lord which would do or dare anything for His sake, regardless of personal cost. Were we contenting ourselves with something cooler, more ordinary, less costly?

Among our young people there was still a spirit of restlessness, even of rebellion, abroad. This was partly a quite understandable reflection of the exciting but unsettling times in which they were living. It seemed that we all needed to be replenished with God's spirit of power and of love and of discipline.

Amma's birthday on December 16th has always been a special Family occasion. Games or expeditions to favourite spots in the near countryside occupy the early part of the day. In the late afternoon the whole Family assembles out in the open for a coffee party. Later in the evening special meetings are often held.

Norman Burns was the speaker at the Birthday Meeting that year and his message was very simple, but it brought us right back to the Lord Jesus Himself. Our hearts were rekindled with love as we were reminded of the absolute sufficiency of His work for us, and of the efficacy of His shed blood to cleanse us from sin, and to keep on cleansing us from those "small" daily slips and failures which we ignore or condone at our peril. Norman talked about our need to walk in the light with the Lord and with each other, allowing no unconfessed and unforgiven sin to remain as a barrier between ourselves and our Saviour or between one and another.

God's work among us was quiet and unspectacular, but we knew that He had met us in our spiritual need. He gave us new vision, new hope and new courage for the fresh problems and tasks that lay ahead of us.

The beginning of this year had also seen us facing an altogether different kind of need.

For several years past our accounts had shown an excess of expenditure over income. This did not mean that we had gone into debt or that we had been without any of the necessities of life. In previous years God had sent us more than was necessary to meet current expenses and so we had a reserve upon which we could draw.

In January 1951 John Risk and some others felt the need of a tangible sign that we were still walking in the way God had chosen for us. He prayed specifically that the financial year might end with a surplus, however small, of income over expenditure. Already in March, because of a legacy which Amma had bequeathed to us, the accounts in fact showed a surplus, but we thought this should be held for some special purpose which God might show, and not be used for current expenses. We therefore prayed that the year's surplus might be over and above the amount of this legacy.

Month by month the accounts were watched with eager interest. God put it into the hearts of very varied people in different parts of the world to send us gifts. A schoolboy in the U.S.A. had been following news of the Family here for some time. He wanted to help the children so he undertook to pray regularly for one of them. His "prayer child" was a boy only a little younger than himself, but he felt very deeply the responsibility to pray for him. At about this time he took his first job—a newspaper round— and in due course sent us the tithe of his first earnings. Someone else in England wrote a rather surprising letter to say she was saving sixpence daily by reducing her cigarette smoking. She would like us to use the money for feeding the poor. April, May and June showed all liabilities met and the amount of Amma's legacy still intact, so John thought he would tell the Family of his prayer, and ask those who felt so led to join in praying too.

Interesting gifts continued to come to us, and we often felt very unworthy when we read the letters that accompanied them. A friend became concerned because she thought our cost of living must have greatly increased. She sent us a very large gift, part of the amount realised by the sale of a property. At about the same time a small boy read an account in one of our prayer letters of the recent drought and famine in the district and of the way the poor people around us were suffering. He read that the Family was forgoing a meal a week in order to give food to the starving, and decided he would like to help. He had set his heart on a very special pair of gum-boots which he wanted for his birthday, but he made up his mind to do without them, and to send the money to Dohnavur instead. An elderly lady had received help from some of Amma's books and she too sent us a gift as a thank-offering.

It was disappointing therefore, and a trial of our faith, when July, August and September showed increasingly large inroads into the legacy. John began to fear he had made a mistake in sharing his prayer with the Family. Suppose the year ended with a shortfall. Would the faith of the younger ones be shaken? Would they feel that God had abandoned us, or that He no longer answered our prayers as all through the years He had answered Amma's?

A heartening letter came from a veteran missionary, enclosing a thank-offering for her husband's safe escape from Communist China. They were folk who, like ourselves, looked to God alone for the supply of their needs, and her letter was full of faith and courage and praise.

Our financial year closes at the end of October. Various figures have to be collected before the full year's balance sheet can be drawn up. December 16th with its meetings and spiritual blessing came and went. In January, in the very first week of the first New Year after Amma's Home-going, the completed accounts became available.

When the whole Family gathered in the House of Prayer on January 18th, John had set out the figures for the year's expenditure and income on a board which was initially covered with a cloth. He reminded them of our prayer, and then began progressively to uncover the figures as they had stood month by month. He was a gifted speaker in Tamil, especially good with young people, and he presented the facts clearly for all to understand. Suspense grew as he explained first the initial surplus, then the shortfall in July, August, and worst of all September, when it had reached a considerable size. Could God possibly give us enough in one short month to balance our budget?

He could and He did. The final figure showed a surplus of just one-half per cent on the whole year's accounts.

None of those who wrote or who sent gifts knew what were our specific needs, neither did anyone outside Dohnavur know of our prayer for a special sign in that particular year. Even we ourselves did not know the exact amount for which to ask, and considerable accounting had to be done before we were sure that our prayers had been answered. Our Heavenly Father knew accurately what our needs would be. Could He have given us clearer assurance that He Himself was still our Guide and our Provider?

We believe that the Lord God omnipotent reigns. It is reassuring to see proof of this in our small affairs, and to find our prayers answered by His working in the hearts of His children around the world.

11

Place of Life

When Meenila was five years old she was promoted from the Nursery School and moved into the Jeevananda, which is the name of the Kindergarten section of the school. Here she began to learn to read and to do sums. The stern business of acquiring knowledge had really begun. She enjoyed her lessons and it soon appeared that she was rather above average in intelligence.

She was an affectionate soul, warm and friendly, and by this time she had quite a large circle of special friends, to each of whom she always remained loyal. Her quick wits and ready tongue, and her capacity to make people laugh, made her something of a leader in her own set. She had developed a great liking for dolls. She would play at families, with herself in the role of mother, and would go through the routine of caring for her "children", bathing them, dressing them, cooking for them and feeding them with meticulous care and absorption. If she could persuade children smaller than herself to play the part of her "babies" that was even better. Thus her inarticulate longing for a mother's love was perhaps reflected in her play. Haleema, one of her close friends, was blessed with parents as well as brothers and sisters living here in Dohnavur. Meenila listened enviously to her talk about them. How lucky she was! How lovely it must be to have a mother and father of one's own!

When she was six years old, Annamai, the Accal in whose care she had now been since she was two, left Dohnavur for a year's experience as a nursery school teacher in a city school. The new India was developing at a phenomenal rate and we were sending more and more of our children to complete their education in schools away from home. If the Accals were to help them adequately and to prepare them to take their place in the larger world, it seemed essential that they too should have had first-hand experience of life beyond our walls.

These Accals had been entrusted with the care of children because their lives gave evidence of their devotion to the Lord Jesus, and because both they and we believed He had called them to that particular work as a life-service. Inevitably their own way of life had, as a result, been adapted to the needs of young children, and their world had thus become a rather circumscribed and perhaps a protected one. Yet to stand up to the rough and tumble of life in a hostile environment can be a valuable and rewarding experience. Anyone whose trust is well and truly placed in the Lord, and who comes through such experience unscathed and enriched in Him, has much to share with others of a personal knowledge of His faithfulness.

Meenila's "set" was now temporarily moved to the care of an Accal named Tarahai who had herself lately returned to Dohnavur from a Teacher Training course. Even though they were assured that Annamai was coming back to them, the parting from her was difficult and unsettling. A year is a very long time when you are only six. They loved Tarahai, but the relationship with her

could not be quite the same as with the Accal who was their
very own.

In 1953, having fulfilled her contract, Annamai returned home
and the little family was reunited amidst great rejoicing. In that
year Meenila had a relapse of her rheumatism, and for months
after it her activities had to be restricted. She could not play
vigorous games, or join the others when they went swimming.
In the evenings when her companions went for strenuous walks
she must content herself with a gentle stroll with the small
children who did not go far or fast. Fortunately she loved them,
and got much pleasure from mothering the tinies; yet she found
the limitations imposed on her very frustrating. Though never
one to complain or to dwell much upon her own ill-health, she
found it hard to be different from other people.

When Meenila was eight, and nearly due to move up to the
Pushpa Stala where the bigger girls lived and went to school,
Annamai began to feel restless and unsettled. Amma had gone.
A *Sittie** who had been in charge of the Square for years, and
whom she had greatly loved, had lately retired and left. She now
no longer felt sure of her own vocation to spend her entire life
serving the children in Dohnavur, and thought perhaps God was
calling her to a different kind of work elsewhere. At the time when
she had first begun to care for children the choices open to her
had been very limited. Young women of her age were not leaving
Dohnavur for employment elsewhere. Had the circumstances
been different she might have acted differently then, and could
not be blamed for wanting a change of work and environment
now. As her children were at an age when anyhow they faced a
move, she did not think that her leaving would harm them at all.

When it was clear that these thoughts were not a passing whim

* The Tamil word means literally "mother's younger sister", and is used in
the Family as a convenient term for our women missionary workers.

due to temporary depression or discouragement, Annamai was helped in her efforts to find a new sphere of service and in due course secured employment away from Dohnavur. God taught her much after she left us, and with His help she made a really valuable contribution in the big high school where for years she worked as a matron. It was inevitable however that her going would have some repercussions here.

Meenila and most of her "set" went back to Tarahai with whom they had lived temporarily before, but now the relationship was a different one because they were to be her own children and to settle down with her.

As Pushpa Stala children they found themselves promoted to various small girls' privileges. Each of them became the proud possessor of a brass food bowl and tumbler inscribed with her own initials. Until now most of their basic necessities had been supplied out of common stock, but now they became women of substance with property of their own, and a private shelf in a locker in which to keep it. Kindergarten days were over, and they began to learn in the big school known as the Jeevalia, the Place of Life.

Quite soon Meenila came to love her new Accal and to have complete confidence in her. Nevertheless Annamai's departure right out of her little world must have made that world seem alarmingly insecure and unstable. Who else might suddenly leave? Did Accals really mean it when they called you their very own children and said they loved you?

For some years now, life followed an even and uneventful course. Then when Meenila was nearly eleven, the Rev. Joe Mullins, a staff worker in India of the Children's Special Service Mission, came to Dohnavur to conduct meetings for the younger members of the Family. The meetings were popular and aroused a lot of interest. All their lives the children had had regular Bible

teaching at home and at school, and were accustomed to attending
Sunday services. Yet now, as is so often the case, to hear the
Gospel presented by a stranger with a new method of approach
made it suddenly come alive.

Mr. Mullins talked about the Passover. He told the children
how, long ago in Egypt, the eldest son in each family was sen-
tenced and condemned. Sometime during a certain fateful April
night, each one would die. What could be done? Was there no
way of escape? Yes, the first-born son could be saved from the
terrible penalty by the death of another. An innocent lamb could
be sacrificed in order that he might live. Those families who
believed that God meant what He said: that judgment would
indeed fall but that the way of escape provided was effective and
sufficient, took steps to proclaim their faith. They sprinkled the
blood of the lamb that had died on the outside of their houses,
and took refuge within.

Meenila grasped the significance of the illustration. For the
first time she really understood that the Lord Jesus had died for
her. For the first time she saw the need to take refuge in Him.
She still had many battles ahead of her, but now her relationship
with the Saviour was a personal and vital one. She had entered
the true Place of Life.

12

Church Affiliation and Finance

Here we must digress from our story of the work of the Dohnavur Fellowship, and of the life of one of its children, to elucidate certain matters of principle and policy about which our friends in the home countries often question us.

The first concerns our relationship with the recently constituted Church of South India.

From the time of its inception in 1947 this bold bid for Christian unity has captured the imagination of the Christian world. By it long-established denominational barriers were broken down, and the non-Christian world was shown a more united Christian front than hitherto. This in itself was a real cause for thanksgiving.

In our area during the few years immediately following the union of the churches many long-established mission institutions were handed over to the Church of South India amidst much rejoicing and goodwill. This generally resulted in a rapid changeover from missionary to Indian leadership, and from mission to church control of finance and policy.

Our Leaders, the Council, and then the Fellowship as a whole, gave much time and thought and prayer to considering what should be our relationship with this new venture, many of the aims and ideals of which were identical with our own.

Amy Carmichael had come to India in 1895 sponsored by the Keswick Convention, and as a member of the Church of England Zenana Missionary Society. She acted on her own initiative in 1901 when she began the work of rescuing children in moral danger. From the beginning she never asked the Mission for money for the support of these children, and as time went on she was joined in her work for them by people from overseas who had no connection with the Mission or even with the Church of England. Moreover the nature of the work often called for difficult decision and swift on-the-spot action. No mission board at home, she felt, could be held responsible for the things she was led to do, often under circumstances that were quite without precedent. She realised that many people thought her and her actions unconventional. So eventually she resigned from the Mission. Thus the Dohnavur Nurseries, later to be the Dohnavur Fellowship, became officially what it was already in effect, a separate entity, evangelical, inter-denominational, locally autonomous in India, and looking to God alone for leadership and all supplies. Her resignation created no breach in sympathy and friendship with the former colleagues of the C.E.Z.M.S. It did, however, widen Amma's circle of friends, as many people of various church affiliations were drawn into partnership in prayer or in some other aspect of work for the children.

Dohnavur is located in what, before the Church of South India came into being, had been a field of the Church Missionary Society, and our relations with that Mission were very happy.

The Family used to attend the village (C.M.S.) church regularly on Sundays, until in the 1920s its numbers increased to the point where there was no longer room for both them and the village congregation to assemble in the one building. The Pastor then asked Amma if she could make some other arrangement for her children. In spite of this change our relation with the church and its life continued to be one of easy, friendly co-operation.

Now, in the early 1950s and in the light of the new changes, it was natural that we should wonder whether or not the Lord would have us forgo our independent status. The matter was looked at very carefully and with earnest prayer, but at length we reached the unanimous conclusion that God was not leading us to make a change. We should maintain our widely inter-denominational position, and still look to Him alone for direction, control and support.

We have continued to enjoy happy fellowship with our near neighbours of the Church of South India, particularly with those of the Tirunelveli Diocese within which we are located. We are indebted to them for much loving help in hundreds of ways, especially in matters concerning the education and employment of our children. We are always glad if in our turn we are able to help them in any way.

We find ourselves in similar happy partnership with many other Christian people of various denominational backgrounds. The basis of this unity is not one of outward observance, but of our shared relationship with the living Lord.

We encourage our converts, and our own children when they leave us, to join whatever group of true believers God may lead them to in their own locality. It is our prayer and longing that wherever they may go, those whom we have taught and shepherded may strengthen the true Church of God in this land.

But no sooner had we unitedly affirmed our conviction that God would have us continue to look to Him alone for the supply of all material needs than He brought us into a time of severe testing.

I well remember the occasion when the reality of the crisis we were now facing first became clear to me. The Council had met, as was customary, in the room that used to be Amma's. Perhaps the words "council meeting" invoke in the reader's mind a picture of carpeted floors, long shiny tables and upholstered chairs, clean blotting paper and a sparkling water carafe. Nothing could be further from the facts where we are concerned. Amma's room contains little furniture except the packed bookcases that line the whitewashed walls. The setting sun shines through the trees and in at the west windows, lighting the red floor-tiles with greenish reflections. In the home-made aviary on the verandah the birds chirp cheerfully and irrelevantly. The council members mostly sit cross-legged on the floor in a large circle.

Our Treasurer, Philip England, was giving us carefully mar-shalled facts and figures concerning our financial position. For many years past, expenditure had exceeded income. The one-half per cent surplus on the last year, though encouraging as a sign, had done little to improve the overall situation. If our income continued to dwindle, and if we continued to draw upon our reserve fund at the present rate, the latter would quickly be exhausted. With dismay I grasped the implications of these facts, and realised how small a margin there was between us and the end of our human resources. At that time the Family numbered nearly a thousand, many of them children and young people, and there was quite an appreciable number of physically or mentally handicapped folk too. Supposing God did not provide for them as hitherto. What could they do? What could we do? What indeed! How lightly I had taken for granted the supply of all our needs in the past, and now in this crisis what a responsibility was ours.

We prayed earnestly and with a sense of overwhelming urgency.

Some wonderful gifts came in, but still the income did not catch up on the shortfall.

In the Council we spent long session after long session reviewing our financial position and our current policies. Sometimes the oppressive heat seemed to match the oppression of spirit that came upon us and that we knew we must resist as we grappled with this problem. What was God saying to us through this time of dearth? Had we embarked on any project which He had not in fact commanded?

The biggest new venture of this time was in the realm of education. Here expenses had soared. Yet we all felt sure that the steps taken with regard to this had been inspired by the Lord, and that we should not retrench.

We examined our standard of living. Was it too high? Were we viewing as essential amenities what were in fact luxuries with which we should dispense? This proved an exceedingly complicated question. Considerations of health and efficiency had to be weighed against the apparent need for economy. We did not feel led to make any major changes in our basic living standards at that time, though some minor economies were effected.

We examined our stewardship of the money God had given us. Was He withholding supplies because He saw in us some sin of pride, some failure in obedience? We asked Him to search us and to show us if there was any such thing.

At about this time May Powell startled the Council by telling us that she felt the Lord had shown her something in which we were indeed disobeying Him.

She reminded us that in many of the children's houses the Accal in charge had a *thungachie*, a younger sister, living with her to help with the housework and many other small jobs. The character of some of these thungachies was far from satisfactory. Had they come from elsewhere and offered for service with the

Family, we should not have accepted them. They were, however, our own children. They needed employment and the Accals needed help. It seemed natural to supply the need from the source available. Theoretically these young girls had no direct responsibility for the little ones, but inevitably their influence was considerable, and often it was not at all helpful.

In the early days of her work for the children, Amma had had some unhappy experiences with workers who were not entirely single-hearted in their motives for service. These experiences, illumined by her study of the Bible and particularly of the book of Ezra, led her to adopt as a principle the axiom "Spiritual men for spiritual work". Yet none of us had thought seriously of our inconsistency in employing these girls in this way until May spoke of it.

Yet the difficulties in the way of remedying the situation seemed insurmountable.

John Risk now told us that God had recently been speaking to him through verses in Ezekiel 44 where Israel is severely taken to task for allowing "aliens" to take part in the Temple ministry. Such ministry should have been performed only by men consecrated to God's service. How could we ignore something which seemed so clearly to be God's word to us? So measures were taken to rectify the existing state of affairs.

All this took time.

We thought and prayed too over the possibility that we were holding back from some forward step that the Lord wanted us to take. No dramatic revelation was given us then of cataclysmic changes we should make. Yet quietly He led us forward into new developments which have proved increasingly important.

In 1951 Philip England, our treasurer, had to spend some months in Great Britain on Fellowship business. In his absence Thyaharaj, the value of whose quietly expressed counsel was becoming increasingly evident, stood in as co-treasurer. This had been a step in the right direction, but a small one; we needed to go further along these lines.

Our Finance Committee meets weekly to make decisions about routine and current expenditure for the Family. In 1952, the year when the question of supplies became such a burning one, three Europeans resigned from this committee and their places were taken by Indians. In the same year Purripu Sargunam* joined the Leadership Group, while Thyaharaj was appointed assistant secretary, and David Aruldasan† co-treasurer of the Fellowship. These two subsequently became and have remained secretary and treasurer respectively.

These steps towards a more equal division of responsibility between missionary and Indian members in our financial and administrative affairs have clearly been of God's appointing. They were perhaps among the advances He was waiting for before answering our prayers concerning supplies.

Another innovation of this time was a scheme whereby some of the more senior members of the Family were to receive a cash allowance from which to meet a proportion or their own expenses. Until now all their needs had been met from common funds. A very small gift on Amma's birthday was the only money they had received individually to handle as they pleased.

It should be added that, during this entire period of straitening, we had not modified in any way our programme of poor relief for the countryside, nor had we reduced the amount of free treatment given to underprivileged patients in hospital.

Towards the end of 1953, when discussions on finance had

* Purippu is the daughter of Ponnammal whose history is the subject of one of Amma's early books: *Ponnammal*, London, 1918.

† His father Aruldasan was the first man to join Amma in the Dohnavur work. His mother's very unusual story is recounted in Chapter XIX of *Amy Carmichael of Dohnavur* by Frank Houghton, London, S.P.C.K., 1953.

recurred with monotonous regularity for a long time and we could see absolutely nothing further to do in the matter, Philip England suggested that the time had come to commit the situation to the Lord and leave it in His hands. He named a certain figure, to which we all agreed, and proposed that if at any time our reserves should fall below that figure an emergency meeting of the Fellowship should be called and our whole position and policy be brought again under review.

From the time of Philip's suggestion, our balance of liquid assets has never fallen anywhere near the figure he named.

In the course of the next two years the allowance scheme was extended until it included practically every adult member of the Family, though the younger ones receive less than those who are older. From the time this scheme was fully implemented right up to the date of writing God has given us a surplus on every year's accounts. Surely this is His seal of approval on the various steps taken during those critical months. Surely too they are His assurance that we may press on in the work He has given us to do for Him.

The Dohnavur countryside from the foothills of the Western Ghats. The
Fellowship homes lie in the distant trees just to the left of the white tower of
Dohnavur village church

Hindu temple gateway

Temple procession
with bearers

Amy Carmichael of Dohnavur—
"Amma" to her children,
December 16th 1867 – January 18th 19.

Meenila in her first year→

←"You can't catch me!"

Cottage families

End of term; High
School girls at a
railway station

Holiday chore,
checking accounts

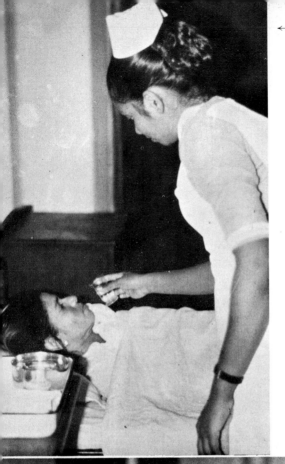

←Nursing trainee

"Jeya Toys" ↓

Labouring woman takes
her children with her
to the fields

Village day-nursery children
at singing games

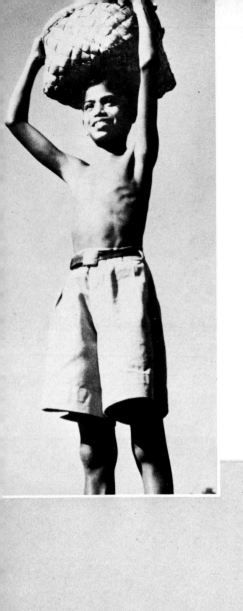

Laboratory technician

Industrial Institute trainees

Dohnavur parents add seven boys to their own
young family

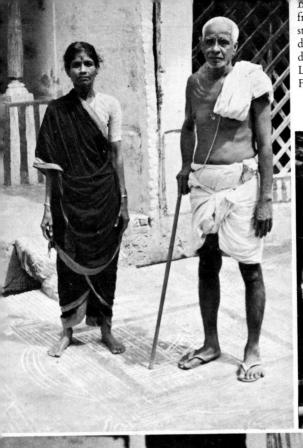

Brahman patients in front of their home stand amid street designs they renew daily in homage to Lakshmi, goddess of Fortune

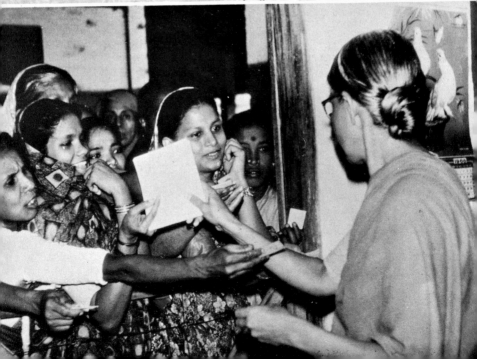

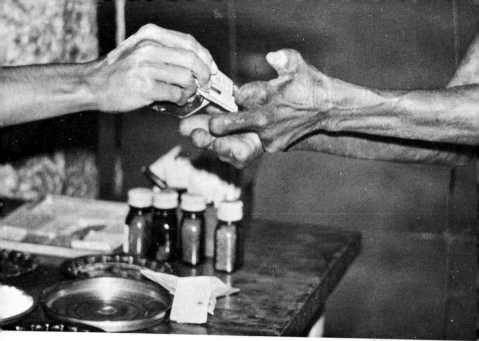

Leprosy hands

Muslim grandmother

A faithful teacher to the end:
Caruniammal, one of Amma's early companions,
herself converted from Brahman widowhood to
Christ, instructs another Hindu widow.

Clamouring
out-patients

D. A. Devapiriam, V. Thyaharaj, G. David Aruldasan, S. D. Rajappan

INDIAN MEMBERS OF THE DOHNAVUR COUNCIL

Saralie and Nesaruthina behind; Christina and Nishka in front: Shantie standing

13

Opportunity

Although our children and their affairs tend to become very absorbing to us, there is always plenty to remind us that we conduct our lives against a Hindu background. We also have a responsibility towards the people amongst whom we are placed, who know nothing of the living God.

Early each morning before it is light the silence is broken by the dreary sounding of a conch shell at the local temple. It is the duty of the local priest to "wake" the god each day with its doleful note.

If we cycle along the road that marks our western boundary we pass a small demon shrine. Beside it there is a pile of derelict idols. They lie there in various undignified attitudes, covered in dust and fouled by passing dogs and scavenger pigs. In former days each of them in turn was the presiding deity of the shrine. People came there to pray to them for such favours as the cessation of a cholera epidemic or the granting of rain. In due course each in turn has been superseded by a more stylish god with fresher paint. No one prays to the discarded ones any more, but neither does anyone seem to find incongruous their present impotence and degradation. It is all too easy to become used to these sounds and sights associated with Hinduism and to forget their implications. Sometimes a chance remark in ordinary conversation highlights the terrible need of those without Christ, and startles us with a renewed sense of the urgency of our commission to make known the Good News of His salvation.

"For about twenty years I longed to hear more of Jesus Christ, but I never met anyone at all who could help me."

The speaker was a Brahman woman who had been brought into hospital very ill a few weeks earlier. As she began to recover she was given, and eagerly read, first a Gospel and then the whole New Testament. We taught her about the Lord Jesus, and she surprised us with her very quick grasp of spiritual truth and her whole-hearted, uncompromising response to His love. We asked her if she had ever heard of Him before.

She told us that when she was about ten years old some women came from Dohnavur and rented a house in her home town. They went around talking about Jesus Christ and selling Christian literature. The Brahmans of her community, especially the men, were extremely angry at this presumption, and they strictly forbade their children to have anything to do with the unwelcome visitors. The house they had rented was put out of bounds; they were to be regarded as out-caste of the out-castes; their literature must under no circumstances be accepted or read.

Our patient, Rajalakshmy, told us that her curiosity and spirit of adventure were thoroughly aroused by all these prohibitions. She could not for the life of her think what harm those inoffensive-looking females could do to her, and she was determined to find out what kind of books they were selling. Accordingly she saved the money given her to buy sweets, and secretly visited the forbidden house on her way to school.

"Give me one of your books," she had urgently demanded, holding out a coin. Eagerly snatching the selected tract she had run off. Concealing it in her lesson books she read it during school, and was gripped by its message. During the next weeks she bought two or three more little books in the same way. Then the Dohnavur women left the village and she knew of no way to obtain further literature, and there was no one to tell her more of the God of whom she had read.

In due course Rajalakshmy reached marriageable age and was withdrawn from school and kept in seclusion in the back regions of her house until her parents could arrange a suitable match for her. She then married and went to live in the distant home of her mother-in-law.

The city to which she went is a rapidly developing centre of large industrial projects. The Christians there are a small minority community, and it is likely that social sanctions would have made it difficult for any of them to contact this young member of an orthodox Brahman household, even had they known of her existence. So her next opportunity to learn more of Christ was afforded by this illness so serious that her husband had decided to take her to her mother's home to see her own family once more before she died. As a last resort her own parents brought her to our hospital for medical aid.

This was in 1956. Our hospital had been open for about twenty years, and there had been medical work from makeshift premises for about ten years before that. The confidence of the countryside was slowly being won, so that by now we had many friends in Rajalakshmy's home town. Even the men, who in her childhood had so strictly forbidden all contact with the Dohnavur folk, now frequently came with their families for medical help. Some of them had read the Bible with interest and were quite ready for long philosophical discussions, though none from her caste had yet openly professed faith in Christ.

Now that Rajalakshmy talked so definitely about trusting Him there was consternation in her family. They had expected her to die, instead of which she had recovered, and her baby, born in the hospital, was alive and healthy too. They saw the hand of God in this. The power of the Lord Jesus, in whose Name prayer had been made, could not now be denied. It might even be perilous to oppose Him. So Rajalakshmy was not hindered.

In due course she returned to her husband's home where she lived quietly as a Christian. She was never allowed to receive baptism or to attend a church, but in her own circle she made no secret of her faith.

Eventually she had a recurrence of her illness, and was admitted into a local hospital of the Church of South India. There, we heard later, she made earnest efforts to win to Christ the other patients in her ward. One night, after she had been speaking to them of Him, He took her during sleep to be with Himself.

Not many patients respond to the Gospel as quickly and decisively as did Rajalakshmy, but the Lord does hear and answer our constant prayer, sending to the hospital numbers of people whom He has prepared to receive His word.

In our evangelistic work both in the wards and in the villages we have found that individual teaching yields greater and more lasting results than do more wholesale ways of approach. This method is, however, very slow and demanding of both time and personnel, and there is obviously a place for other strategies too.

The return from their places of training of some of our senior hospital staff, and the arrival of several new recruits, made it possible to reopen the men's out-patient department in 1951, and the men's wards in 1952. From that time on the medical work grew and developed year by year. The wards were always full, and the out-patient department fully extended, but there were villages not so far distant where the Gospel was still virtually unknown and we began to consider what further steps we could take to reach them.

For a time we tried running "road-side dispensaries", using our motor van to visit some remote spot each week with a medical team. About every six months we changed the rendezvous, but it did not take long for news to get around, so that there was usually a good crowd waiting for us when we arrived. During the afternoon's proceedings there was always an opportunity for somebody to give a short Gospel address to those gathered for treatment. We generally held also a meeting illustrated by lantern slides in some other village on our way home.

In 1953 we opened a small medical out-station in a village where we had friendly contacts through grateful patients. This approach to the evangelistic problem we planned as a "combined operation". The resident nurse and her companions had many opportunities to visit the women in their homes and give them personal teaching. They also ran a popular Sunday School which was regularly attended by almost all the children of the village. We doctors with a hospital team took it in turns to visit this centre for a weekly clinic. We held the usual Gospel meeting for the patients, and afterwards went on to other places for further open-air witness before returning home.

Sometimes patients invited us to take our slide-projector and musical instruments to little hamlets right off the road among the endless groves of palmyra trees. With the stalwart help of our brothers, who always organised and led this part of our activities, we reached in this way places to which we women might never otherwise have penetrated.

On one such occasion our goal was a village of the so-called Robber Caste. At first the villagers somehow mistook our car for the police van, and since discretion is the better part of valour there was not a man to be seen in the place by the time our party disembarked. However, their scouts must have informed them of their mistake, for they soon re-appeared and attended the lantern service with interest and the greatest goodwill.

During these years the rapid increase of literacy, and the tremendous demand made by the youth of the country for reading matter, presented a new challenge. Communism was hastening to fill this need, and so too were the publishers of lurid, sexy paperbacks who found an expanding and highly profitable market for their wares. Some of the men of our Family tried in a small way to meet the challenge by making a drive to distribute Christian literature more widely in our district. They organised several ten-day tours in our motor van, each covering a distance of from one hundred and fifty to three hundred miles. During each tour they sold many thousands of books, Bibles and portions of Scripture, held meetings, and had many opportunities for personal witness to their customers.

Every new venture was a cheer and encouragement, but to us it seemed that we were reaching only an infinitesimal fraction of the teeming crowds around us who were still without God and without hope.

14

On to Higher Education

The longed-for monsoon had broken and rain was pouring down in torrents. With open umbrella the Sittie due to take the next school period in the Jeevalia battled through the downpour and the mud and arrived in her classroom to find her pupils having a wonderful time out in the open courtyard. One of them, drenched through, was Meenila.

This is a not unusual reaction to the first arrival of the season's rains; but remembering Meenila's rheumatism and her many long spells in hospital, the Sittie lost no time in calling the girls to order. In no uncertain terms she told them what she thought of them for getting soaking wet like that. Meenila came in for an extra scolding.

This was exactly what she had wanted. Here she was getting a large share of attention from Sittie, who was obviously really worried about her. Had she not, by her example, incited the others to play in the rain, Sittie might not have specially noticed her at all.

In these days her naughtiness often took such a turn. She had a great longing, as had many of her contemporaries, to be the centre of attention and to have somebody's love all for herself. The many changes of Accal she had experienced in her short life, and the fact that she had never known a mother's care and the security of a father's protection, probably had much to do with this subconscious craving for proof that she was loved.

Meenila had had several more attacks of rheumatism and her heart was permanently and quite severely damaged. Her physical activities were officially restricted, but whenever she could escape supervision she rushed about with the other children, doing all they did and more if possible. She had joined the Bulbuls (the Indian equivalent of the Brownies) and later the Guides. This had provided some outlet for her energies because here there was much in which she could join with others on an equal footing without undue exertion. In school too she was definitely bright and had kept up with the other children of her own age in spite of the many interruptions caused by illness.

She could use her hands as well as her head, and so was potentially a very useful person; but she was still hot-tempered, and was beginning to be noticed for her too-smart retorts when corrected or reproved. This sometimes made her seniors hesitate to ask for her help.

With her own set it was different. She was such good fun that everyone loved her. She was loyal to her friends, and would never let them down.

Holidays came, and with them the opportunity for new and exciting games. During one long holiday Meenila and her friends developed a craze for cooking. They had a little fireplace of their own on which they could practise to their hearts' content. There were various popular sweets that could be made out of bananas and jaggery (unrefined palm-sugar). Meenila would begin a cooking project with the greatest enthusiasm, mixing the ingredients correctly and putting the concoction carefully on the fire; but then, like all children, she wanted it to be finished at once. She could not be bothered to stand stirring it, and waiting for the slow business of boiling. Sometimes she would run off to play, leaving her sweets to cook themselves. If the result was a charred mess, that was just too bad.

Like all our children she was taught to interest herself in the world of nature around her, the gay hoopoes that wandered eccentrically about the grass lawns of the Square, the noisy flying foxes that came at night to feed on the margosa fruits, the translucent geckoes skilfully hunting moths and flies on the cottage walls, the massive green-gold beetles with their slow, lumbering flight among the flowers, the silvery chrysalids that hung hidden under the lanceolate oleander leaves.

One day her Accal found her operating on a cocoon with a needle. "I am doing Karunai Sittie's work," she explained. "I am helping this lazy butterfly to come out quickly." (Karunai is my Tamil name.) She exposed the beautifully folded embryo to the light of day, but was surprised and disappointed when it failed to fly and she found her impatience had killed it.

By 1959 Meenila was thirteen and was well up to standard with her school work. It was time for her too to emerge from her cocoon and stretch her wings. Had it not been for her ill-health she would certainly now have gone out to boarding school with the other girls of her own age. But as yet there are no special schools in this part of India for children with physical disabilities such as hers. We doubted her ability to cope with the rough and tumble of life in a big boarding school where no one has the extra time or the special knowledge to give a delicate child individual care. We therefore reluctantly decided to keep her at home at least for another year.

This was a big disappointment to Meenila, even though she had had her own private misgivings about leaving home. It was hard to see her friends going off to the sewing-room in excited chattering crowds to be fitted for the new outfits they would need for school. She moped around the house, wishing there was an excuse for her too to have new clothes. It was hard not to get irritated also by her friends' endless spirited arguments about the relative merits of the different schools they were going to. Haleema was bound for Madura, a hundred miles off. She knew a good deal already about the enormous Pierce Memorial High School because she had had a sister there, while another sister was even now on the school's secretarial staff. No other school, she was complacently sure, could possibly hold a candle to this one. Meenila's special friend, Revathi, with equal confidence, was about to join the Sarah Tucker High School in Palayamkottai. Anihala, who was very shy, was due to accompany her and looked forward to the new experience with mixed feelings. Dear old Usila, always the butt of so much teasing, was contentedly going to Megnanapuram.

At last the talk was over, the preparations completed. The hand-cart loaded with tin trunks made its positively last journey to the bus stand, and the last group of curiously subdued and suddenly homesick girls said goodbye, boarded their buses and were borne away to their destinations. The new phase of life had begun.

By this time our educational policy was stabilised, and much that at first was experimental had now become routine.

It had become our standard practice to send the girls on to boarding schools as soon as they had satisfactorily completed seven standards in our own schools. The boys begin attending the Walker High School in Dohnavur Village at the same stage, and then, after one year, most of them are also transferred to boarding schools. We put both boys and girls as far through high school as they are able to go, endeavouring to equip them to earn their own living and fend for themselves. We feel it immensely important that they should be as free as possible to seek God's guidance for their own lives, and that there should be no pressure put on them to return to Dohnavur for permanent service. We do not want them to come back unless both they and we are quite sure that God Himself has called them to do so.

This does not mean that we do not want, or need, recruits. We constantly pray that God will call and equip young people of His choice from among our children for the work here.

As I have already said, in the early days we ran hostels for both the boys and the girls attending high schools. After a few years it became impracticable to concentrate all the boys in one school and all the girls in another. The hostels were therefore closed and the children were dispersed in Christian boarding schools all over Madras State.

Every year, because of the increasing numbers of Indian parents seeking education for their children, it becomes more difficult to obtain admission to the schools with a good academic record. God has been very good to us in giving us many kind friends in the different educational institutions who have helped members of our Family in countless ways, and particularly in this matter of allotting them vacancies.

This increasing emphasis here in Dohnavur on academic achievements is not to imply our whole-hearted approval of the present public examination system. That system, as a recent critic has observed, tends to encourage, not sound learning (in the sense of the thinking through of problems) so much as the acquisition of hastily memorised information on a variety of standard classroom subjects. "In recent years the rush for professional degrees such as engineering and medicine has been intense because of their economic value. The system as it prevails today, therefore, has lost its religious, cultural and philosophic moorings, and has even cast adrift its humanistic idealism. Even the simple pursuit of truth through the investigation of scientific or other knowledge is in danger of being lost to all but a chosen few. The result has been the lowering of standards in the quality of education as a whole."*

In giving priority to Christian character-building therefore Amma was, we believe, placing the emphasis where in education it always should be placed. Nevertheless today the School Leaving Certificate, the technical diploma, the university degree, are the passports to employment. The present need therefore was a much tougher one—to see Christian character developed in our young people, not in a sheltered school life here among us, but in the wider setting of a strongly competitive system, and if necessary in spite of the sheer materialism of many of its standards.

Accordingly, when in due course some of the senior boys and girls who had passed well out of high school began to ask for university education we considered and prayed over the matter in some detail. Various questions suggested themselves to our minds. Was it right to spend on just one person's education so much of the money that God entrusts to us for general use? Further, if we were to decide that the privilege of higher education might indeed be extended to some, should it perhaps be limited to those who definitely intended to return to serve in Dohnavur? And again, what sort of standards should we demand of anyone asking to be allowed to proceed to university?

Eventually we decided that it was part of our mission to train people to serve God and their country in key positions anywhere in India, not only here in this work. We felt that any to whom

* S. P. Appasamy, "The Christian Colleges in the Life and Witness of the Church in India", *National Christian Council Review*, Mysore City, October 1966, p. 405.

this privilege was given should have shown their academic calibre in school and have attained a good aggregate of marks in their School Leaving Certificate. Furthermore their characters should be such as to give confidence that they would use their special qualifications for Christ in whatever work they might take up after graduation.

Since this decision was made, three students, two men and a girl, have taken up the study of medicine. The senior man graduated in 1963 and is now in charge of a small Christian hospital, where he has great opportunities for serving God. Several others have tried for places in a medical school but have been unsuccessful, and have had to enter slightly less competitive professions. In all, three more young women have entered university to read for Science or Arts degrees. Several young men have done the Pre-University Course successfully and have proceeded to advanced technical studies in such subjects as engineering, pharmacy, pathology and bacteriology, while others have gone on to take degrees by private study.

These young people at university have shown that they have a useful contribution to make to college life. One at least has gained honours for her college in the field of athletics. They have all linked themselves up with the Union of Evangelical Students of India (affiliated with the International Fellowship of Evangelical Students). Most of them have been office bearers in its branches and seem, as far as we can tell, to have given a positive witness for Christ among their fellow students. For all this we give humble thanks to God.

15

Urgent Problem

"They told me 'Education is not for girls'!" The old lady almost
spat the words at me. Temporarily a patient in hospital, she was
very aristocratic and well-mannered, but her feelings were roused
now, and she let me know it. What use was it my giving *her*
books? She had never been taught to read. She had, it seemed,
begged when a child to be allowed to go to school, but had been
told that her duty was to marry and have children. "I was very
young when they married me," she continued, "and my husband
was much older. I had no children. Before many years had passed
my husband died. Then one after another my parents and both
my brothers died too, but I lived on. Who wants a childless
widow? I had nothing; no husband, no children, no parents, no
friends and," she added with great bitterness, "no education
either."

It was horrifying to think of the bleakness of my friend's life;
the round of small menial household tasks, the scornful glances
of more fortunate folk who had escaped the tragedy of early

childless widowhood, the long empty hours of stark boredom, unrelieved by even a book or a paper.

"Education is not for girls." That had been the common view in this part of India at the time when Amma's first children were in their growing years. Quite emphatically Amma had not agreed with it. Right from the beginning she had tried to give her girls a liberal education along lines that were original and sometimes unconventional. Above all things they were encouraged to read, and in order that the scope of their reading might be widened, they were taught English as well as Tamil from an early age. Consequently in some ways their outlook and horizons were far wider than those of the average village woman in the surrounding countryside.

There the conviction that education is not for girls affected far more than mere schooling. During the early decades of the century it still coloured people's thinking to such a degree that career women, already making their influence felt in the north, were virtually unknown in this remote southern district. The idea was unthinkable here. Only very poor women worked for wages alongside their husbands and brothers on the land or at any unskilled manual labour at which they might earn a pittance. The life of such women was harsh, and they were despised by the more fortunate leisured classes.

Further off in the great cities and at the other end of the social scale, things were, as I have said, rather different. There were some women of character who had gone through high school and on to university, even entering the professions. Many girls educated in mission institutions became nurses and teachers. A few of the most progressive even took their part in pioneering revolutionary social reforms in their country. But here in the conservative south an unmarried woman who offered any kind of social service in a country town or village would have found her motives, and even her moral integrity, suspect by the people of her village. Marriage was considered the sole purpose of a woman's existence. Yet marriage itself was hedged about with rigid customs and conventions which could not be evaded.

All marriages were arranged. Sometimes an irrevocable arrangement was completed while the couple concerned were still children. Caste, family connections, compatibility as directed by the horoscope, these were the determining factors in most such arrangements. Even among Christians few parents were sufficiently emancipated from time-honoured customs to ignore caste and family relationships entirely when negotiating marriages for their children. This then was the social background within which Amma's older children arrived at an age when they must seriously consider their own future. Amma has left it on record that from the beginning she hoped and prayed that all her children would render service "of value to the Lord, for India". But by the time the first of them were entering adult life her Family had grown to an extent that she had never envisaged. In every part of it she badly needed more and more dedicated full-time workers. She was determined to act on the principles God had shown her and to accept as colleagues only those who were one with her in aims, convictions and loyalty to Him. So she prayed for recruits from among the grown-up members of the Family. Who better than her own children could help her to continue and extend a project intended only for God's glory and the good of India's children? Many of them responded to the challenge of the need they could see and understand so well, and joyfully undertook whatever task they were given for the Master's sake.

Those however who had no clear call from God to the work here, or who were not entirely in sympathy with its principles and the goal towards which it was directed, found themselves in a difficult position. Suitable employment away from home seemed virtually unobtainable. Many of them would have welcomed marriage, but as orphan girls they had no family connections from amongst whom a bridegroom might be expected to materialise, and the motives of young men who looked for brides outside their own circle of distant relatives were not always above suspicion. Amma discovered this by bitter experience. In the early days she lacked an Indian man of mature judgment and experience to give her help and advice, and this increased her difficulties in negotiating marriages for her girls. In spite of her most careful preliminary enquiries some of those she did arrange turned out unhappily. Eventually she became rather disillusioned, and grew chary of accepting any offer unless the young man's credentials were good beyond possibility of mistake. In consequence, for a considerable number of years very few of the girls married at all.

It thus came about that, whatever their outlook, for good or ill the great majority of the women of the Family remained here in Dohnavur. There was plenty of work for them to do within the big community, and those to whom the highest spiritual aims meant little and who could not be received as fellow-workers in the fullest sense were occupied with "things" rather than people. Cooking, sewing, handwork, weaving, cleaning, laundry work and gardening, all were necessary for the common good. Some of the folk so employed found quiet satisfaction in work well done, in developing their own particular skill, and in sharing in the corporate life of the Family. Others were restless and dissatisfied. The relationship of these latter to the rest of the community often gave cause for grave anxiety, but at first they comprised only a small minority within the whole.

Years passed. Slowly and almost imperceptibly the nation's opinions and customs began to alter. Then with the coming of Independence in 1947 and with the development of the Government's campaign for literacy in the following years, the country was abruptly jolted off its old lines of thought and custom and tradition. Progress and change began to be greatly accelerated.

About ten years after the above conversation with my illiterate widow friend, I paid a visit to a family who often come to hospital and whose home is in a neighbouring town. Their house is old, and is built according to the traditional plan dictated by orthodox Brahman culture. The doorway is intentionally low, to remind all who enter to exercise fitting humility and to stoop towards the earth from which, it is said, all life springs. Every part of the long narrow house has a religious or philosophical significance of ancient origin. But this was 1964. The family who live there have moved with the times and their outlook is in keeping with modern trends. When I was comfortably settled on a swinging seat suspended by chains from the rafters, one of the girls produced her *tamburu*, tuned it, and prepared to play. Her eager young face was alight with intelligence as she first explained the elements of the classical *ragas* in which she was specially interested, then played and sang to illustrate her points. For the past three years she had been studying Carnatic music at a college in Madras and now she was qualified both to perform and to teach. Her mother, seated on the floor, looked on with quiet satisfaction. She was a woman perhaps ten or fifteen years younger than my illiterate widow, and had herself been allowed five years of schooling before her own, albeit very early, marriage. Now she and her husband were determined that all their daughters should have a full high school education and then go on to a further training after that. "It may be expensive," her husband declared, "but it is a good investment. If when they marry anything should happen to their husbands, they will not be left destitute, but will always have a means of livelihood."

Times had indeed changed! Perhaps forty or fifty years had

passed since the widow had been told that "education is not for girls". Now education for girls and careers for women have come to stay.

In the matter of education God had so led us that our Family also had progressed with the times. Most of our girls were now being given a high school education and, whenever possible, a further training too. The young folk were on the move. The majority of them had left home and were making their own way in the world. In fact during the ten-year period 1955–64 nearly one hundred and fifty girls and women left Dohnavur for employment or marriage, or both. This figure is about six times greater than the total number who left for similar reasons in the previous ten years. That so many of our girls and women were satisfactorily placed was a notable answer to prayer.

It was also the fruit of much painstaking research. During the years when our educational policy was evolving and being worked out in practice, Margaret Wilkinson, Barbara Trehane and others spent a great deal of time and energy exploring the possibilities of further training and employment for girls such as ours. They corresponded widely and travelled extensively throughout Madras State investigating hopeful openings. The result of all this research was to show that the various branches of teaching and nursing, dispensing and hospital laboratory work offered the best prospects to girls with a good education but without a university degree. Shorthand, typing and accountancy also have limited possibilities and will doubtless soon come into their own as skills in which women can excel and be employed with profit. University graduation, of course, opens up many more avenues to interesting and profitable careers, but so far few of our girls have measured up to the academic standards required for this.

To know the goals towards which to work and the routes of approach to those goals is good, but even this is only half the battle. Competition for entry to training institutions is tremendously keen. For teacher training there may be as many as a thousand eligible candidates applying for forty places. Vacancies in State colleges are allocated on a communal basis, and even in Christian colleges fifty per cent of the selected students must be non-Christians. There are only three such Christian training colleges here in Tirunelveli District, but God has greatly helped us in the difficult matter of securing places for those eligible.

Then when it comes to employment new problems arise. Although the India of our times is greatly changed, acceptable openings, even for well-trained girls, are still hard to find. Not only is there competition for every post with good prospects. Employers tend now to demand constantly rising standards of education. Moreover girls with no family in the background have great difficulty in finding suitable living accommodation. As yet hostels for working girls are rare, even in the large cities. Convention forbids an unmarried girl to lodge in the house of any but a close relative, unless the establishment is an all female one. This means that our young girls can only take employment in institutions where quarters are provided for women residents.

If the placing of the academically successful is so difficult, what of those who through lack of ability, ill-health, failure to exert themselves, or some defect of character, have come out of school without a satisfactory School Leaving Certificate?

These indeed present a great problem and a challenge to prayerful effort.

In 1959, having exhausted all obvious sources of information on this subject, Margaret went to Madras to consult there with some of the heads of big social service organisations. She asked them what sort of employment they found for the orphan girls in their care, particularly those with little education. The women concerned were kind and sympathetic, but they were very gloomy about the prospects for such girls. They made few suggestions and could give little information that was new to Margaret. The problems are clearly not peculiar to our own work.

Here in South India there are Government sewing examinations for which people can prepare who have had only an elementary education. These qualify successful candidates to teach sewing. There are also courses of training for auxiliaries in nursing and midwifery. People holding certificates of this type cannot command a very good salary and there is little hope of promotion, but such qualifications are better than none. There is, alas, very little else available.

Each year that passed had made us increasingly aware how necessary it was to help all our grown-up boys and girls to find congenial work away from Dohnavur, unless both they and we had an unmistakable assurance that God Himself wanted them to stay and serve Him here on the home team.

It was more than ever clear to us too that the group of young women here now who had failed to make the grade academically badly needed a new start in fresh surroundings. Yet with the meagre openings available, how were we to meet this need?

Moreover, in addition to these young folk, there was also a quite large group of older women within our walls who were really misfits. Their presence here was a direct result of the days when public opinion had been so strongly against girls' education, and when at the same time marriages had been so hard to arrange. Many of these, as they now watched younger folk profiting from their studies and leaving home, became themselves increasingly dissatisfied with their circumstances and their jobs. All too few were prepared for the costly personal sacrifices that work for children properly demands. Many resented the discipline necessary for the smooth running of so large a community as ours, and craved the greater personal freedom that independent employment elsewhere might give. But there were also a few who wanted security without responsibility, and who were content to remain within the Family, receiving all it had to give without making any adequate contribution in return.

In a work geared primarily to meet the needs of children and those caring for them it became increasingly difficult to cater for this large mixed group. Yet since they had had no formal state-recognised qualifications the task of placing them outside Dohnavur seemed almost impossible.

During the years following Amma's death the very size and complexity of the Family began itself to present baffling problems. Besides the administrative difficulties inherent in so large a group, the presence among us of a number of adults who were careless of our most vital aims made it hard to maintain the kind of home atmosphere we coveted for our children.

That the Family had ever been allowed to grow quite so large was perhaps a mistake. Circumstances had been forbidding. The seemingly great barriers to any other course had hemmed us in. Even so, a more accurate appraisal of the changing attitudes in India, and a determined effort to take advantage of them at an earlier date, might well have found an acceptable way to disperse the misfits sooner and so to help them forward to a more congenial way of life in other spheres. Amma and her colleagues of earlier days would be the first to admit their own fallibility. We who have followed after, and who have gained immeasurably from their example of single-minded devotion to God, as well as their undeviating sincerity in seeking to know and do His will in every detail of life and service, are in no position to criticise. We may have been more aware of modern trends, but many of us know ourselves to have been far behind in spiritual maturity. Now at length developments which Amma had never foreseen had overtaken us. They challenged us to seek God's face afresh, that

He might lead us into new ways commensurate with the gravity and urgency of our newly felt needs.

By the late 1950s the affairs of these two groups, the older folk who were misfits and the younger ones who had failed to use their educational opportunities, had become for many of us a major preoccupation. What could we do to help them find a satisfying and profitable way of life? How too could we reduce the numbers of those living in Dohnavur, and at the same time weld the essential Family here into a more integrated whole?

With considerable effort posts were found for a few of the older women, who gladly moved out to become housekeepers, storekeepers, wardens, matrons and helpers of different kinds in schools and other Christian institutions. Some of the less able went into domestic service. Whatever their faults and failings may have been, most of the latter have won a reputation for good hard work, kindliness and honesty. This last is a sufficiently rare commodity to have created quite a demand for women from here to fill this kind of post, especially in households where there are children or old people to be cared for.

As has been hinted earlier however, the social structure of this part of India is such that posts of the kind just mentioned can be taken only by older women.

Each post found was a valuable move in the right direction, but at first the number who were benefited seemed pitifully small, and the Family still remained much too big. Clearly we needed to take other and far more drastic steps to decentralise the work if our troubles were to be adequately tackled. But what could those steps be?

By the year 1959 the magnitude of the problems facing us, and the impossibility of the situation in which we growingly found ourselves, were casting us back upon God in a way that lesser difficulties might not have done, and the experience enriched us.

16

New Look, New Projects

If acceptable tailor-made jobs were not waiting to fit the requirements of our girls and women, was it then our duty to set about
creating some for them?

During the years 1955 and 1956 Thyaharaj had run a hostel in
Madras city for some of the young men. There are sometimes
great difficulties in finding work for them too. This difficulty is
not due, as with the girls, to lack of outlets, or to custom and
social sanctions, but to the high incidence of unemployment in
the State and the resulting keen competition for every vacancy.
This makes failure at school for any reason whatever a very serious
thing for the lads. Some of the senior Annachies have travelled
many hundreds of miles in their search for suitable employment
for one boy or another, and their correspondence on this subject is
voluminous.

At the time when the hostel was opened there was a group of
young men in rather special need of help in their first plunge into
the whirl of city life. While they completed courses of training,

or gained their initial experience as wage earners, Thyaharaj made a home for them and helped them in a thousand ways. About thirty young men passed through the hostel, and then it had to be closed. Thyaharaj was badly needed at home, but it was clear to us that during the seventeen months of its existence the place had fulfilled a most useful function.

Several years later, as we considered the needs of the different groups of our women, we began to wonder whether a similar hostel in a city centre might be useful to some of them. We visualised something run on slightly different lines. It was unlikely that the girls we had in view would get outside employment or would be attending courses of study. It was thought however that they might work at, and support themselves by means of a suitable home industry. Soft-toy making had recently been developed here and some of the young women were already engaged upon it. This seemed to offer possibilities. Employed in this way they could at the same time learn to cook and keep house, to budget for their own needs, to keep accounts and tithe their money under realistic conditions of town life. They could be initiated into the subtle skills of marketing and the more serious economics of a small business. They could discover from experience the relationship between hard work and living standards. They could participate in the life of a local church and develop normal friendships and contacts outside the protecting circle of the Dohnavur Family.

In the simple, natural setting of the small hostel, unsupported by the herd instinct that may sway a larger group, they could think through and apply lessons learned from childhood but not till now made fully their own. Perhaps too their personal spiritual needs could be understood and met in that informal atmosphere, as they had not been met in the bigger community.

Barbara Trehane planned and initiated this project.* At the beginning there were so many obstacles that someone less determined and less sure of God's leading might easily have felt the whole idea was a mistake and abandoned it. The site chosen was Bangalore, the capital of Mysore State, a city with fast growing industries and a million population which included, in a mainly Kannada language area, a fairly large Tamil community. She began by searching the city for a suitable house at a suitable rent. After innumerable interviews, official and unofficial, and after quartering the widely spread and hilly city on a bicycle for weeks, she was completely unsuccessful. The Hindustan Aircraft Company was expanding its factories, and hundreds of new workers were pouring into the city. All were seeking housing and rents were prohibitive.

Then, when the situation looked quite hopeless, a large legacy was received in Dohnavur. The sum was sufficient to cover the purchase of a house. The Leaders wrote telling Barbara of this timely gift and suggesting that God was leading us not to rent a house but to buy one. This altered the position entirely. Barbara found two or three likely houses, Philip England went to Bangalore to give expert help with the final choice, and soon the legal formalities of purchase were completed.

In the autumn of 1959 Barbara and an Accal called of God to share in guiding this project, moved in with the first group of young women, and the toy-making began. At first they met with much discouragement. There was a trade slump in Bangalore. Shops which had earlier been anxious to buy toys sent all the way from Dohnavur itself were now having great difficulties in moving their stocks, and some were even closing down. They could not place any new orders with "Jeya Toys."

* She has described it more fully in a booklet, *Ordinary People's God*, London, The Dohnavur Fellowship, 1964.

Things indeed looked black and forbidding for the small business.

Barbara did not find it easy to maintain the morale of her group, but inspiration was given. She devised a competition in toy designing which captured their interest and aroused fresh enthusiasm. Some of the workers showed surprising skill and ingenuity, and produced models that have continued to sell well ever since. A popular toy was the noble and incomparable pig, Count Curley Wee, popular hero of a serial comic which has run daily for very many years in the Madras *Mail*.

Gradually trade improved, new customers were found, and the toy industry flourished. The Accals in charge (a second one joined the staff in 1960, and now there is a third) never have an easy task, since the workers they train constantly change. Again and again newcomers have to be taught right from the beginning the skills of the trade, the neatness, the speed and the technical craftsmanship.

Eventually Barbara was able to leave the Accals to run the hostel on their own, with just an occasional visit from her to give help and advice on business and other special matters. Left to themselves they, and particularly the senior in charge, have learned to walk very closely with the Lord. The little family under her care has had many opportunities to prove God's faithfulness, and has experienced some truly wonderful answers to prayer. In a very marked way the girls have learned the joy of giving. They have opportunities to witness for Christ, and, in helping and teaching others, have learned valuable lessons themselves.

Most of the forty girls who have passed through Jeya between 1959 and 1964 have gained in maturity and poise besides acquiring a lot of useful know-how. Fifteen of them have gone on to training courses, nine into employment, and seven have married. Six have come back to Dohnavur enriched by their experience and sure of their call to work here. Only three have remained unsatisfactory, and are back here in Dohnavur, employed, but still dissatisfied.

In the main the Bangalore hostel filled a need by providing training for young women. There remained however the middle-aged group for whom little was being done.

By 1959 we had become increasingly aware of the countryside's changing outlook towards social work and women social workers in particular. This change is due in part to the spread of the influence of Mahatma Gandhi and the practical implementing of some of his very far-seeing ideas.

As an important part of its Five Year Plans the Central Government has divided the country into zones. Trained personnel are appointed to develop the natural and economic resources of each zone, and to provide various social services for the population of the area concerned.

As part of this Block Development programme women are given the opportunity to attend courses in cotton spinning and are encouraged to work at it on a co-operative basis. They can also receive instruction in the use of the sewing-machine, in dress-making and in other simple handcrafts. Women social workers run day-nurseries for children of pre-school age whose mothers are poor and must work all day in the fields. The idea is to utilise every possible source of profit to the country and to help people to help themselves. Where they co-operate and make constructive efforts of their own, the Government may supplement their resources with grants in kind or with cash subsidies.

For every village that has an organisation of this kind, there are still very many where nothing is being done to help the poor, and no social services exist. Could we, we wondered, exploit this need for social workers and the public's new attitude towards them as a constructive outlet for training and employing some of the rather difficult group of middle-aged women within the Family? Many of these people possess loving and sympathetic instincts that are largely dormant and unfulfilled. If only we could overcome their initial reluctance to leave their comfortable rut, they might discover undreamed-of happiness in a piece of useful service thoroughly in line with the most modern trends of their country. Were they to undertake this as a commission from God, great opportunities for evangelistic work and personal witness might open up.

After much prayerful planning Olive Fuller piloted the new scheme in the village of Pannaivilai. This is in fact the village from which much of Amma's earliest evangelistic work was done.* Between 1960 and 1964 Olive took forty-three women through a simple course of training in Pannaivilai lasting one year for each trainee. The village is, on the whole, poor. Olive and her students adopted a standard of living similar to that of the majority of the villagers so as to make vital contact with them easy. They ran a day-nursery, earned a little money by spinning, taught others to spin and to do simple sewing, and held adult literacy classes.

Most of her trainees were surprised, and at first horrified, to find how much they themselves had to learn. One result of our sheltered community life had been that to them village customs and etiquette had largely become a closed book. They found shopping and housekeeping on a limited budget not nearly as foolproof as they had thought. Green-fingered gardeners seeking to supplement the diet or brighten the place with flowers encountered unimagined opposition from the goats, fowls and cattle of the village.

Most of them enjoyed to the full their participation in local

* Descriptions of Amma's early work in Pannaivilai will be found in *Amy Carmichael of Dohnavur* by Frank Houghton, London, S.P.C.K., 1953. Olive Fuller has written a more detailed account of the new training work in *Better to Give*, Chicago, Moody Press, 1965.

church life, and were soon drawn in to help with the various activities of the C.S.I. congregation. They undertook also some Sunday school work on their own account.

As they went about their daily tasks those passing through the training found themselves confronted with much very urgent need. This awakened in some of them a true desire to help. Several discovered as a consequence that they had never allowed the Lord fully to meet their own spiritual needs. Because their own wills were yet unyielded to Him they lacked the power to lead others into life, liberty and victory. Some invited the Lord to deal radically with the causes of their previous failure, and now discovered a new joy in His service.

Each year since the inception of the Village Training Centre, a new subsidiary centre has been opened in a different locality. These centres are all being run by women trained in Pannaivilai, and they are making a good job of it. Their chief contribution in each village is the running of a day-nursery, and this has proved to be very popular. It is appreciated not only by the children's parents but also by the school teaching staff, who formerly had often themselves to provide unofficial baby care.

Other trainees have returned to Dohnavur with a new vision and a new sense of vocation, and with an acceptable contribution to make in the Family. Sadly, there are still others who have failed to respond to the training, or to be challenged by the material and spiritual poverty they have seen at such close quarters. The best that can be said for these is that they are more fitted than formerly to look after themselves and to find useful employment away from home.

The village centres are meeting a need very acceptably. There is no doubt of this. There have been more invitations than we could accept to send workers and to open day-nurseries in various villages. We who have watched the project develop and who know the people engaged in this work constantly thank God for what He has done for them. This is the Lord's doing and it is marvellous in our eyes.

17

Coveted Objective

In 1960 it was decided that Meenila should have her heart's desire and be allowed to go out to boarding school. She was desperately keen to continue her education, and to obtain the certificate which is the "open sesame" to various training courses and careers.

The school selected for her is a large one with a good reputation for academic attainments. In view of her poor health, it had the additional merit of being not far from home. Although the school is under Christian management, a considerable percentage of the students are Hindu or Muslim, while the Christianity of a proportion of the rest is a matter of name rather than personal conviction. In such a setting Meenila was due for a lot of new experiences.

As always with each fresh group of children who launch out into this new phase of life, we saw them go with mixed feelings, and many were our prayers for their future well-being.

In any school the "new girl" must stand up to a barrage of questions when she first puts in an appearance.

"How many brothers and sisters have you?"

"Are both your parents still living?"

"What work does your father do?"

When it is discovered that our children have no parents, they come in for a lot of gratuitous sympathy and commiseration, which they often find very hard to bear. Some of them had never thought of themselves as orphans before, and the way the other children regard them is most unwelcome, somehow giving them a feeling of inferiority.

There are usually some people in the school who have heard a little about Dohnavur, and sooner or later someone will suggest that the parents of the Dohnavur children are likely to have been people with none too good a reputation.

"Didn't your own mother love you enough to want to keep you herself?" they ask.

"She must have been a very bad woman," someone else will insinuate.

This kind of talk, though more often thoughtless than deliberately cruel, is quite enough to shatter a sensitive child's security, and cause a serious emotional upheaval.

Freed from close supervision for the first time, the youngsters encounter many problems in connection with their money allowance and their personal property. In Dohnavur there is little difference between the value of things owned by different children of the same age-group. We have everything we need, but there are not many luxuries as judged by the standards of the wealthy. When they go out to school, the children's outfits are planned to be in line with the average for the institution concerned, so that they shall not be made conspicuous by being noticeably different from other children.

At a school like the one Meenila now entered, some of the girls have many valuable possessions. Expensive watches or fountain

pens, lavish silks and jewellery can be a source of great temptation
to our children when they see them in the possession of their
classmates. Covetousness and discontent can be fed by the nagging
thought, "If I had parents I could have these things too".

The other girls from poorer homes have often seen the hard
work and sacrifice that have made their own education possible.
They know that privileges are dearly won, and if they have to be
careful and economical with their money, the reasons are not hard
to understand. Our children, on the other hand, know nothing of
poverty. They are told of the sacrificial giving that lies behind the
supply of their needs. They know something of the wonderful
way God answers our prayers in such matters, but it is hard for
them to envisage either their indebtedness to the givers or their
own practical dependence upon God. It seems to them that the
Leaders of the Fellowship can tap inexhaustible supplies at will,
and many of them go through a phase of thinking it is only
essential meanness that withholds from them luxuries of every kind.

Reaction against the disparaging talk about orphans leads some
of them to assert their importance by disbursing their allowances in
the grand manner. They may then be tempted to reimburse
themselves by a little private trading of books or clothes or other
possessions. Others go into debt. (This is considered a very
respectable thing to do in this part of India. The reasoning is
that if people trust you enough to lend you money you must be
the right kind of person.) Some few others have adopted more
definitely dishonest methods to make good their losses or to
supplement their resources.

Monetary muddles occasion many headaches and heartaches in
the holidays when the boys and girls have to produce their
accounts and their belongings for inspection. In the end valuable
lessons are learnt by most of them, but the process of learning
can be painful.

Personal relationships are another pitfall when they first leave home. Here in Dohnavur all the school teachers are older brothers and sisters of the Family, and when the boys and girls go out to school they find it hard to establish a normal teacher-pupil relationships with the new school staff. This is not by any means always their fault, though they may sometimes err on the side of familiarity. The obviously high-caste origins of many of them make them interesting and attractive to inexperienced young teachers, and as a result they are sometimes badly spoiled. Sooner or later they will unwittingly presume on such privileged treatment and thereupon suddenly find themselves out of favour. This of course strikes them as unjust and inexplicable. Conversely some teachers think that orphan children have no one behind them to care for them, and so they make them the scapegoats for everything that goes wrong in their class or in their boarding home.

Covetousness was not one of Meenila's failings, and her innate honesty kept her from getting entangled in money troubles of any kind. Neither did she become involved in difficult relationships with members of staff. She was an attractive child but not a strikingly beautiful one, and this may have been some protection to her. She on her side was not specially drawn to or interested in any of her teachers, but regarded them quite impersonally.

Meenila's experience of the Lord Jesus had not gone very deep yet. She had seen and believed something of His love for her and had trusted Him for the forgiveness of her sins. But she was definitely still at the receiving end of things spiritual.

It had not yet occurred to her to give anything costly to the One who had given so much for her. She had even lost something of the wonder of her first experience of Him, and He seemed now to her unreal and very far away.

Sometimes children whom we have failed to lead to Christ

have found Him while at boarding school. Others have had their
faith strengthened, and have witnessed bravely for Him there.
Some have received positive help from members of staff and
others with whom they have come into contact at school. For
Meenila it was otherwise.

It was not that she got into any serious trouble with the school
authorities, or that she failed to co-operate with those at home
who deal with the schoolgirls' affairs. It was just that she was
influenced by people whose criterion of conduct was different from
anything she had met at Dohnavur. They were modern, up to date,
emancipated from old-fashioned ideas. To them success, money,
popularity and pleasure were the supreme values. The Bible was
all very well in church on Sunday but could not be regarded as a
guide in the ordinary affairs of daily life in this twentieth century.
The questions raised by these new ideas were frequently the
subject of discussion among our schoolgirls when they met again
at home during the holidays. Some were prepared to go the whole
way with their new friends. "Why should we be different from
other people? Even if we are orphans we can still have a good time
and do what everyone else does," they declared. Some few stood
staunchly by the Bible teaching they had had at home. For her
part Meenila thought this had been a bit extreme and narrow.
Perhaps the Sitties were mistaken in some of their views. After
all they were foreigners. What could foreigners know of life in
modern India? The Accals were getting old (in her estimation);
they too could easily be mistaken. It would never do to be old-
fashioned and odd.

Nevertheless, the ties with home were still strong. Along with
the other "Dohns", as they had come to be called in their schools,
she eagerly looked forward to the weekly newsletter. The frequent
personal letters from her own Accal were more welcome still;
and when in her first term an Accal visited the school it was

indeed a red-letter day. Meenila was as eager as the rest for news of everyone and everything at home. She looked forward with excitement to the holidays, but she was also quite glad to return to school when they ended.

Half-way through her second term there was a 'flu epidemic in the school. Few of the girls were very ill. Most of those who were had only two or three days in the sick-room, then returned, none the worse, to normal life. Meenila got it too, but she rapidly became seriously ill—and quite frightened. She was thus relieved beyond words when, after some days, the Dohnavur car arrived and took her home to bed in our own hospital. Now of course she would be well very soon. She had no doubt she would be back at school in time for the Christmas celebration at the term-end. She was bitterly disappointed therefore as the days lengthened into weeks and she was still kept lying flat in bed, unable to do anything that really interested her. To make matters worse, Tarahai was temporarily away from Dohnavur and so unable to help by visiting her in hospital.

The Christmas holidays came and she heard of the doings of her friends. Some of them went on a camping trip with Barbara Trehane to one of our houses in the mountains. Tidings reached her of the tremendous fun they had there, exploring, swimming in the river, playing adventurous games in the jungle. Morning and evening they met for times of Bible study and free discussion, times that meant much to some of the girls who took part in them. From all these activities Meenila felt terribly cut off.

There were days when her patience wore very thin. Then, resentful at life's unfairness, she would give her nurses a bad time with her unco-operative behaviour. She was tormented with the question that has bothered many far older people. "Why should this happen to me? Why am I always prevented from enjoying the things that other people do? Why?" Yet in spite of this she usually managed to keep her inward conflict to herself, and to present a bold face to the world.

We who cared for her were also troubled by a haunting question: What of the future? What had God in store for Meenila?

18

Frustration

It was in April 1961, after six whole months in hospital, that Meenila was considered fit enough to leave the wards and return home. She was very nearly fifteen years old. She looked terribly fragile and delicate, but the firm set of her jaw proclaimed her determination not to recognise any physical disability in herself.

Tarahai was back in Dohnavur again, and the holidays were in full swing once more, so Meenila's home-coming was thoroughly happy. As her convalescence had progressed and she had come to feel really better, she had thrown off some of her dark doubts and fears. When she got back among her own set and to her own Accal, she slipped easily into the old childhood ways again, and the reactionary mood of her brief schooldays was temporarily forgotten. She did not confide it even to Tarahai.

Yet she was still sometimes tempted to resent it when everyone else joined in some exciting activity in which she alone was unable to take part. It was like that when the schoolgirls went off for their traditional picnic to the river up in the foothills. They were

out from before light until sunset, and came home full of stories
of their swimming prowess, the fire they had lighted, the cooking
they had done, the songs they had sung, and the people they had
met on their long hike. It was tantalising too not to be able to
take an energetic part in the programme when the girls put on a
display of Indian games and folk dances for the entertainment of
the rest of the Family. There were, however, quite a lot of things
she could do, and she was soon once again a ringleader in her own
set. There were other interests too. With the rest of her friends
she thoroughly enjoyed the documentary films that were shown
each week during the holidays. This was a treat made possible by a
friend's kind gift of a sound-track cine projector.

During these holidays a special series of Bible classes was held
for anyone who wanted to be prepared for Baptism. Meenila had
not previously taken this step, and now she asked if she could
attend the classes. She found them immensely interesting, and her
experience of a few years earlier, when she had asked the Lord
Jesus to be her Saviour, took on for her a more profound significance. On Sunday, May 29th, along with some of her special
friends, she was baptised. This step of obedience to her Lord
seemed to bring with it a new and overflowing joy.

Though the decision cannot have come as a surprise to her,
Meenila was deeply disappointed when she was told that she was
not to return to school that year. Arrangements were made to
coach her privately for the Elementary School Leaving Certificate,
which would have been her goal in the next academic year any-
way.* This was a great comfort to her. Even if she must stay at
home while everyone else was away, she was not losing valuable
time, but could still keep up with her classmates.

In other respects things were not so good. When the others had

* New regulations now demand that this examination shall be taken only
from recognised schools.

all left for school, she found life flat and uninteresting. Never fully fit, she found that little things irritated and annoyed her. Constantly her thoughts turned to the life she had tasted but never really savoured in her short months away from home. She longed for a little excitement to brighten up her rather uneventful existence.

Then suddenly the blow fell. An energetic staff worker was needed at our out-station at Pavilions. Tarahai was asked if she would be willing to move out there to give the needed help.

Pavilions is very beautifully situated in the southernmost foothills of the Western Ghats, only about ten miles from Kanyakumari (Cape Comorin). It has an exceptionally healthy climate, and we have used it for years as a home for girls and women who, whether from physical disability or mental handicap, can neither keep up with the competitive life in the big Dohnavur Family nor earn their living independently in the larger world. In the small group there they can receive individual help, while life proceeds at a pace suitable to their capabilities. Part of each day those fit for it do some agricultural work, growing useful crops such as ground-nuts and gram.

An industry has also been developed for them and they spend most of the rest of their time working at this. They extract the fibre from a type of aloe which grows easily and profusely in the locality, and use it to make a variety of attractive articles which find a ready market in Madras and elsewhere. The various processes of this industry demand different degrees of skill and intelligence, so there is something for everyone to do. The work is creative, and the good sales give the workers a satisfying sense of achievement.

Tarahai prayed over the suggestion made to her, and agreed to take up this new appointment with its fresh and very different opportunities and responsibilities.

The thought of the impending separation distressed Meenila, but she understood the reason for it. Her Accal had not lost interest in her, and her motive in leaving her was no selfish one. She was going because God wanted her to help the Pavilions Family. She would still be within reach, and it would be possible to write to her often and see her sometimes. To Meenila the burning question was, "Who will take care of me now?"

This was indeed a big question. Several different people were approached, but they were all reluctant to receive Meenila into the circle of their other children. The trouble was her habit of clever repartee. They were afraid that if they had to correct her for anything she would answer back in such a way as to make them look foolish in front of the other children. Or she would parrot their tones with just the right amount of exaggeration to make mockery of the whole incident. This can be disastrous to discipline and is no light thing for anyone to face. Meenila had never behaved like this with Tarahai whom she truly loved, but others had smarted under her ridicule.

Somehow Meenila came to hear of the difficulty. She was completely devastated to discover that she was not wanted. This was stark tragedy indeed. Yet it was a salutary shock.

When a young Accal named Nesaruthina, a graduate who had only recently returned to take up work here, offered to accept her, Meenila was overjoyed. She was prepared at once to give her all the love and devotion of which her passionate little heart was capable.

Nesaruthina was already coaching her in some school subjects, so she was no stranger. She quickly won Meenila's confidence and respect, and never had any trouble with rudeness. She too had known the allurement of some of the world's compromising attractions, so Meenila found it easy to talk to her, and to discuss with her all the questions that were churning through her young mind. Nesaruthina well understood the restless longings and the conflicting loyalties. She had gone through it all herself. She had been among the first nine schoolgirls to go to Trichy, and later had had six years in college in Madras, followed by teaching experience in a high school. Now she lost no opportunity of turning Meenila's thoughts towards the Lord Jesus, in whom she herself had found the answer to her problems and a satisfying purpose in life.

Meenila listened to all she had to say, but she was on the whole better at talking and expressing her own views than at taking advice. Besides, she had developed another preoccupation.

For hours every day the communal loud-speaker in the village just over our wall blared and blasted out its programme of music and news items. The music predominated, and consisted mainly of recordings of the latest cinema songs. They are played over and over again until everyone within earshot knows the catchy tunes by heart, and most become thoroughly saturated with the sentimental, sugary words as well.

Meenila loved these songs. She was quick to pick up both words and tunes. They excited and fascinated her, till gradually they became an obsession. She sang them morning, noon and night, and quite lost her taste for any other type of song. When Nesaruthina gathered her little family together for prayers at night and taught them a new hymn or one of Amma's lovely children's songs, everyone joined in with enthusiasm. Meenila alone would have none of it. She shut her mouth determinedly and refused to take any part at all. Somehow, without realising it, she was slipping away again from her Lord. Yet she was unable to find true satisfaction without Him: for in spite of her constant, enthusiastic singing she was very far from happy.

19

Matters Matrimonial

It was hot. The peace of Sunday afternoon had descended on the red-roofed houses among the margosa trees, and most adults were flat on the floor enjoying a brief but welcome siesta, when a messenger came hurrying to Margaret Wilkinson's house with a reply-paid telegram. It was addressed to "Missionary Lady, Orphanage Home, Dohnavur", and the message read: "Required Protestant Bride aged over thirty for marriage Bridegroom Bachelor aged thirty-nine employed Government Service New Delhi reply." The sender's name was quite a common one and of course there was no address for reply. History was repeating itself, but in a fresh context.

After a few days an express letter arrived supplying a few more details concerning the thirty-nine-year-old aspirant to marriage, and administering a mild reproof for the failure to reply to the telegram.

The bachelor had a job that took him for various lengths of time to places throughout India. He had therefore decided that an orphan girl with "no encumbrances" would be a suitable life partner. In this context "encumbrances" probably meant a family who might call upon her for help in an emergency, and whom she might want to visit from time to time. He had heard that Dohnavur had "good religious girls" who were given in marriage to eligible suitors. He stipulated for a good cook who had had a high school education. He wanted the marriage arranged at once while he was on special short leave in the south.

Margaret did not produce the unencumbered, high school educated, Protestant cook by return of post, or indeed at all. The matter ended with an interchange of letters.

The arranging of marriages for our girls is one of the more onerous and least enviable tasks that fall to the lot of our leaders. Sometimes, as in this case, the prospective bridegroom introduces himself. More often an intermediary writes on his behalf. Exhaustive enquiries are then begun. If the man's credentials appear sound, and if there is a girl who wants marriage and who also fulfils his stated requirements, she is approached. She is told the known details and asked to think and pray over the offer. If she wants to proceed, the young man and his sponsors are invited to come to Dohnavur. If the sponsors and our Leaders are satisfied, a meeting is arranged between the couple themselves. If they like the look of each other, the marriage will be arranged. This may be the only occasion on which the two meet until just before the wedding, but this procedure is in line with local custom and etiquette.

The "Marriage Bureau" used to be the special responsibility of Rajappan and May Powell. Margaret understudied May for some years, and has now taken it over. It is perhaps unnecessary to say how much she and Rajappan need prayer that God will constantly give them His own wisdom. They frequently have to make decisions, normally made by parents, which irrevocably alter the whole course of other people's lives. Sometimes when enquiries are made it is immediately obvious that the man is unsuitable. An obliging young postman wrote that he had come to "understand that there are so many Secondary Grade Teachers in your fellowship, and I am decided to marry an orphan from your fellowship". This arrangement was certainly intended to be financially profitable for him as the bride was obviously expected to teach. He said that he was "expecting" his promotion to the clerical cadre. There was nothing however to indicate that its imminence rested on any surer basis than his expectations. He also said that, although he belonged to the Hindu community, he was willing to be baptised "anywhere".

For this man to marry a Secondary Grade Teacher would be a step up in the social scale and would also provide easy money. His reasons for seeking a bride outside his own family circle and community were not hard to see. The Secondary Grade Teachers were not lined up for this offer.

Sometimes people's letters are very deceptive. On one occasion a very plausible letter came from a man who wanted a Christian bride. He worked, he said, on a tea estate. He gave the name and address of the estate overseer as his referee, and everything he wrote seemed straightforward and honest.

It happened that some of our married girls and their husbands who lived in roughly the writer's area were badly in need of help and fatherly advice. Rajappan decided that he would visit them, and then go on and meet this prospective bridegroom. Accordingly he set out on a journey that was to prove to be all of six hundred miles. He sorted out some of the difficulties of the families he visited. In one case this involved seeing the officers of the church to which the couple belonged, as well as other villagers who had been entangled with them in extensive and rather serious disagreements.

At last he was free to go on to the estate. The journey took much longer than he had expected and it was quite dark when he reached the remote little settlement. Here he had a series of very odd encounters which cannot all be told here, but which reached their culmination when, in the grey light of dawn, his correspondent left him alone in the house with a weeping woman at his feet. "Sir, sir," she sobbed, "don't bring another woman here to be my husband's second wife."

This man, tired of his legal first wife, had written to Dohnavur in the belief that orphanage officials would readily accept an offer of marriage for one of their girls without checking his credentials. The estate overseer did not even know he had been cited as a referee.

There are times when we are more than ordinarily grateful for the wise help so unassumingly given by our Indian brothers, and this was one of them. Although times are changing, it is still very necessary to find out just why a man is seeking a bride outside his own connection.

It may of course happen that, when a prospective bridegroom seems unquestionably a man of integrity and entirely suitable for one of our girls, there is in fact no one among them to meet his requirements and standards. A young pastor wrote that he was looking for a bride who would be both one with him in spirit and also his intellectual equal. He hoped for a graduate who would be able to help him in translation work which was a special interest of his. We do not have many graduates and the only one we had at that time had other ideas for her future.

On the other hand, when a missionary wrote recently on behalf of an Indian Christian family known to him, their needs and ours exactly fitted each other. They wanted for their son a bride whose interests and education would be on a par with his. He was a para-medical worker in a Christian hospital. A happy arrangement was concluded with one of our trained nurses who had been hoping for marriage.

Sometimes the young man concerned has had some contact with other members of our Family, and is inclined to ask for a bride with the same background and traditions. In Bangalore some marriages have been the outcome of the favourable impression made by the girls of the hostel upon those who have observed them going about their ordinary affairs.

It is equally possible, and terrifyingly so, for the behaviour of members of our Family out in the world to ruin other people's prospects of marriage or of employment in their locality.

Generally speaking, a good education and some further training greatly enhances a girl's marriage prospects. By far the majority of men who enquire here for brides want a girl who can earn a reasonable salary. The previous chapters therefore have a great deal of bearing on this question of matrimony. Success in training, and then in obtaining and keeping a job, often leads on to a happy marriage arrangement. In the past ten years about sixty of our girls have married, and most of these marriages have been arranged from here according to customary procedure. The majority of these, sponsored in a way reminiscent of customs long abandoned in the West, nevertheless turn out very happily. In just a few cases, especially among the nurses, a happy match has been made in a way more in line with practice in the West, and in such cases too our Leaders have of course been ready to sponsor and advise those concerned. But there is now also a growing tendency among educated young people, able to meet profession- ally and socially in a way that members of the more conservative rural society cannot, to try to manage their own affairs. One or two of our own young people have so acted, high-handedly spurn- ing all proffered help. Alas, through ignorance and inexperience some of these have been imposed on and have landed themselves in great difficulties. In the setting of this locality at the present time, it does seem that in general the customary way of conducting these affairs is still the best for most girls and women.

The girls who marry continue to regard Dohnavur as home. Most of them write often and want to receive the monthly news letter. It is the usual custom for young married women to return to their mother's house for their first confinement. Our girls generally adhere to this custom and of course we are equipped here to help them. So we have the privilege of supervising the debut of lots of little grandchildren. This shared joy serves to forge new bonds between us.

In the crises of life they turn to us for help. It may be unemployment, or debt, or quarrels with in-laws, or illness, or some other unexpected disaster that calls for a letter, a visit, permission to come home for a long stay, or occasionally for financial help. Certainly as far as the Fellowship is concerned, although the marriage of our young people may solve certain obvious problems, it also creates a whole lot of new and more complex ones.

It is encouraging to know of a growing number of our girls, as of our boys, who with their partners are bringing up their children in truly Christian homes. By their consistent witness some of these young couples are making on their environment a real impact for the Lord.

20

Clouds and Darkness

At the last moment the brother scheduled to take the English Service on Sunday, February 25th 1962, found himself unable to fulfil his engagement. As so often happened, John Risk quietly and unobtrusively stepped into the gap.

The subject he had chosen for meditation, the verses he read and his brief but illuminating comments gripped his hearers. Few of them had any idea that he had prepared for the service at extremely short notice. His message was fresh and telling, its theme unshakable confidence in God. Here is its outline.

"The Lord reigneth; let the earth rejoice; let the multitude of the isles be glad thereof. *Clouds and darkness* are round about him righteousness and judgment are the habitation of his throne." Psalm 97 : 1, 2.

Clouds and darkness; do they not often mean doubt and fear to us in our spiritual lives? Yet in the Bible both clouds and darkness are often used to show the presence and glory of God.

The clouds show us the rainbow. God used the cloud to guide His people. God spoke to the disciples out of a cloud, and when the Lord Jesus comes again it will be "with power and great glory" in a cloud.

What about the darkness? It has some obvious advantages. Is it not true that in the darkness we walk more carefully and are more willing to be led? The Bible teaches us some other truths about darkness too.

God is in it. "Moses drew near into the thick darkness where God was."

He knows all that is in it. "He knoweth what is in the darkness."

He has in it hidden treasures to give to us. "I will give thee the treasures of darkness."

There is an end set to it. "He setteth an end to the darkness."

John's messages always came out of his own experience. Some of us knew that the last years had often held much cloud and darkness for him. Even as he spoke he was in the midst of a situation that to him was bewildering and painful in the extreme. Nevertheless his faith in God never wavered. At the end of the service he read Knox's translation of Isaiah 50 : 10: "Who is here that fears the Lord, listens to his servant's message? Who would make his way through dark places with no glimmer of light? Let him trust in the name of the Lord and lean upon his God." To trust thus in God was the settled practice of John's whole life, and he never doubted there would be a glorious end of the darkness and a triumphant entry into light.

How soon his own release into unshadowed light was to be given none of us suspected.

On Tuesday, February 27th, John went about his work as usual. He led the Fellowship Prayer Meeting in the late afternoon, and we prayed for the senior boys and the men of the Family. While the urgent needs for prayer he brought to our notice were many, he left us with the impression that there was too a very great deal for which to praise God.

In the early hours of the next morning the men who lived next door to John sent someone tearing to hospital on a bicycle with an urgent call for medical help.

But John did not need our help. He was already in the light of the Lord's immediate presence.

Some few years earlier John had been sent to Britain for medical consultation. He had been told his heart was in a precarious condition, but that with care and the avoidance of undue stress and strain he might still have many years of life before him. He decided that "care" meant the extra discipline of cutting out some of the violent exercise he had till now enjoyed by way of recreation. "The avoidance of stress and strain" however was hardly compatible with his position as Leader. He decided to overlook that ingredient of the prescription and to carry on as usual. Those of us most concerned knew all this. We tried to spare John, but he was ultra-conscientious about bearing his own burdens, as well as about taking his share of other people's.

He made so little of his physical disability that we sometimes forgot how grave it was.

Way back in the 1920s when still very young in years though surprisingly mature in spiritual experience, he had resigned, at its outset, a promising career in the Navy and come to India to join the Fellowship. He had become in course of time an able adjutant to Godfrey Webb Peploe, and had always followed Amma's lead with the utmost loyalty and devotion. The deaths first of Godfrey and then of Amma thrust John himself into leadership in a way he could not have foreseen, and would never have sought. They did so just at a time of world-wide unrest and of political and social revolution in India. With increasing clearness John saw how to relate the world situation to missionary strategy, and the changes in India to the future of the work for the children. He recognised that the evolution of events called for revisions of method. Yet he was scrupulously careful to guard principles that were based on the authority of the Bible, steadfastly shunning any step that savoured of mere expediency without that authority.

As I have tried to show, in the years following Amma's death we all became growingly aware that the very large size of the Family had become a hindrance to the more important aspects of its work. The basic aim lying at the very heart of that work is that all the boys and girls may come to know the Lord Jesus as their personal Saviour and Lord, and that growing to spiritual maturity in Him they may give their lives to His service. But mature Christian character cannot be mass-produced in a pro-tected environment. Our large numbers militated against both the adequate shepherding of individuals and their toughening to meet the storms of life.

As Leader, John had a large share in formulating and putting into practice the various moves that have already been recounted. The most important of these was the reducing, by decentralisation, of the numbers actually resident in Dohnavur and the forming of smaller administrative units.

Although he was thus deeply involved in all parts of the work, John Risk's special care and concern was the teen-age boys and the men of the Family.

The provision here of a home for boys came in 1918, many years after that for girls and women had been established. The number of men and boys in the Family has never been more than roughly one-quarter of the total. Perhaps because men who are utterly devoted to the Lord can exert such a wide and powerful influence for good, this part of the work has always seemed to be fiercely attacked and contested. Basically the joys, sorrows and problems that fall to their lot are just the male counterpart of those already touched upon in the earlier chapters of this book. Possibly boys suffer even more deeply than girls from the lack of parents and of a normal home environment.

The background of our children and the traditions and thought of the local, predominantly Hindu countryside make it necessary to have separate living accommodation for boys and girls from an early age. Therefore at the tender age of eight our little boys pass out of the Accals' hands into the essentially male world of the Vanacharbu and the care of Annachies. These men give themselves in unselfish and devoted service for their sets of boys, and the dedication of some of them over the years has been splendid beyond measure. All the same the absence of a woman to care for them in the home, imposed on us by the social situation around us, has seemed to emphasise the deprivation the boys suffer as orphans.

Much thought and prayer has been given in recent years to measures designed to compensate for this. For long Norman and Lorna Burns lived in the Vanacharbu, and Lorna did much to mother the large family of boys and men of all ages. When for health reasons these two were obliged to retire, Jack and Barbara Trehane moved in to fill the gap and to share the life of the lads in every possible way. Then at about the time when the Bangalore girls' hostel and the Village Training Centre for women were launched, a new plan for the small boys was pioneered. The next set of them due to leave the Accals who had mothered them from babyhood, and to move up to live with the older boys, were transferred instead to the care of Rajappan and his wife Nuranie. These two took them into their own home, which is just opposite the hospital across a public road and some minutes' walk from the Vanacharbu. They have cared for them along with their own children ever since. This has proved a happy arrangement.

Within the ensuing two years two other groups of boys moved to the town of Tirumangalam, nearly a hundred miles to the north of us. Here two married couples, themselves members of the Family, acted as foster parents to them. The families soon became absorbed into the life of the town, attending the local school and taking their part as members of the congregation of the small Christian church.

A scheme that is worth while seldom goes through without difficulty and opposition, and this was no exception. Perhaps the boys chosen for this initial experiment were the wrong age to be uprooted and transplanted, and at first some of them found it very hard to settle down in their new environment. Part of the plan had to be abandoned, but valuable lessons have now been learned which should make future moves of this kind easier as provision for them becomes possible. In the meanwhile the boys left at Tirumangalam seem to have adjusted to the new way of living, and to be making satisfactory and happy progress.*

Concurrently with these changes our educational plans had been developing. John and his team worked just as hard as their opposite numbers on the women's side to place the boys in school and training, and then to find employment for the young men who needed it. There was with us too a small population of younger and older men more or less permanently resident in the Vana-charbu and its adjacent married quarters, men who had stayed on or returned to work in Dohnavur and who were concerned with its farms and gardens and the maintenance of its buildings, services, transport and power-supply, as well as male hospital nurses and technicians and of course the Annachies caring for sets of boys. For the welfare of these John was ultimately responsible and he was actively interested in all that concerned them, from their

* In 1965 this group moved to the town of Cheranmahadevi (Shermadevi) near the new boys' hostel (see Chapter 25).

food and living quarters to their work and recreation in which he loved to join. When important decisions had to be made, even if the final decision had to be his own, he always tried to act in collaboration with the other seniors.

Latterly however a group of men and boys, including some trusted fellow-workers, had become very critical of certain steps he had felt led to take that concerned personnel. Eventually, when after prayerful consultation with others he was regretfully obliged to ask one young man to resign from his place of responsibility in the care of a set of boys, this group violently opposed him. The result was a sharp division in loyalties among the men and a serious breach of unity which had unexpectedly wide and serious repercussions in the Family as a whole.

This was a source of very real cloud and darkness to John. Right to the last day of his life he worked and prayed for a reconciliation with the dissident elements and for the recovery of unity at the deepest level. He did not live to see the answer to his prayers.

This situation was not an easy one for a new leader to inherit.

God led us to appoint Philip England to the general leadership, with Jack Trehane in charge of the boys' side of the work. Jack had worked in close co-operation with John Risk for many years, and was thoroughly conversant with the boys' and men's affairs. Both Philip and Jack had been behind John in the various steps he had taken from time to time. Now as they took up their difficult tasks, each had the confidence that he did so at the direction of the Lord God upon whose shoulders all government rests.

Philip had considerable administrative experience. He had piloted us through the troubled waters of new legislation relating to such things as the possession and cultivation of land, the sales tax chargeable on the products of our home industries, and the taxation on medicines sold in the hospital. An engineer by profession, he had planned and constructed many of our major buildings, and in this capacity had had much to do with the outside labour we employ. In all his contacts, whether with workmen or Government officials or at home with the members of our own Family, he is always on the alert to commend His Lord and win men to Him. Though never so designated he has in fact for years been general business manager for the Fellowship. He has acquired a fund of knowledge of legal matters and of the ways of officialdom that again and again have stood us in good stead. In this last he has had an able and scarcely less gifted colleague in Thyaharaj.

When John died, Philip had already given thirty years of service to the Family. In the last ten years or so the volume of business he was obliged to handle had increased to such an extent that we felt he was already doing the work of two or even three men. Now he must assume the additional heavy load of the work's overall leadership.

Circumstances seemed perplexing. Clouds and darkness threatened to obscure our onward path. Here then was our opportunity once more to "trust in the name of the Lord and lean upon our God". The situation might baffle us. It had not passed out of His control.

21

Satisfied

The death of John Risk had a profoundly disturbing effect on Meenila. From talk in the Family she gathered that he had died of some kind of heart disease. She had already deduced the fact that it was heart damage that had caused many of her own troubles and that was the reason for the long and tiresome restraint upon her activities.

Annachie had gone so suddenly. Would her own end come like that, without any warning at all? Often Nesaruthina would wake in the night to find Meenila sitting beside her, unable to sleep because she was so frightened. She would talk to her and try to comfort her, and usually, after they had prayed together, Meenila would settle down peacefully.

In spite of all her emotional and psychological difficulties, Meenila had done well in her studies during the year. In March 1962 she sat for the Elementary School Leaving Certificate examination which she passed. She very much hoped that now she would be able to continue her education through high school and eventually sit for the Secondary School Leaving Certificate. She knew exactly what she wanted to do afterwards. She would take a Teacher Training course, and then find employment in some city school. She wanted independence and the opportunity to savour such excitements and pleasures as the world might have to offer.

Yet her continued ill-health seemed destined to thwart her ambitions. None of us felt she would stand the stresses and strains of boarding-school life. It did not seem fair, either to her or to the school authorities, to take the big risk of allowing her to return there. Needless to say this decision, when she heard it, produced violent resentment in poor Meenila. There were no more examinations she could take by private tuition, so not unnaturally she felt her doom had been sealed. Her hopeful plans had received their death warrant. Out of sympathy with many of the principles that governed the Family's life here, and that debarred her, it seemed, from the very pleasures she most desired, she yet saw no escape from them. She felt trapped. With teen-age melodrama she declared "They are killing me by keeping me back from school."

It indeed seemed unlikely that Meenila would ever again leave the sheltered life of the Family. Understandably therefore she was discontented, inclined to rebel against her fate and against authority. Both the circumstances over which she had no control and the natural restlessness common to teen-agers conspired to reinforce this attitude of mind. Would she join the ranks of the disaffected misfits? Or would we be able to reclaim her for Christ and introduce her to the joy of serving Him in ways within her physical capacity? The next years would probably be crucial. She became a special target for prayer among those who knew her well and understood her difficulties.

A little later in that same summer of 1962 her emotions

were stirred in a new way, and she experienced yet another frustration.

There was a wedding in the Family. The bride was not so many years older than Meenila herself, but she had done all the things Meenila would have loved to do. She had passed successfully through high school and had gone on from there to a Nursery School training, and then taken a job. She had recently come back to Dohnavur prepared for any service, and now He had opened up for her this way of marriage to one of our own young men.

Meenila was deeply moved by the wedding ceremony, and she discovered overwhelmingly strong desires in herself that until now she had not known existed. Desire was not her only emotion, there was also a horrible fear. Was this another privilege she could never experience?

Eventually she summoned enough courage to face the worst, and asked her Accal the all-important question: "Shall I ever be able to marry?"

Poor Meenila. Her troubles were no longer those of a child. They were of an order calculated to rob a far maturer and more experienced mind of its peace.

She begged now to be allowed to continue to study even though she could not return to school or take further state examinations. Arrangements were made for her to attend a few of the classes that were held to coach people who had failed the S.S.L.C. examination and were preparing to take it again. She enjoyed this, and quickly picked up some of the subjects that were new to her.

Then a fresh prospect opened. In the Kindergarten at that time there were several children who were backward, and finding it hopelessly difficult to keep up with the others of their own age. Meenila loved little children, and had wanted to teach, so it was suggested to her that she might take on this group and help them through their difficulties by giving them individual coaching. This was right up her street, and she was delighted to do it. She found the work interesting and rewarding.

The rest of her time she spent helping a young Accal who was employed in book-binding for the schools. In this she proved a reliable and accurate worker, and soon made herself useful in the department. She enjoyed using her hands, and got on well with her colleague.

As time went on Meenila's affection deepened for her own new Accal, Nesaruthina. With it however a more selfish desire for her exclusive attention gradually developed until it altogether possessed her. She became bitterly jealous of anyone who claimed any of Nesaruthina's time or made demands upon her love. Though excusable perhaps in someone confronted with the difficulties Meenila had to face, this made for endless trouble among the other girls living with her in the house. She became more and more unstable emotionally, and her obsession with the sexy cinema songs of the daily public broadcast was still a major factor in her life. Nesaruthina longed to be able to help her more, but the extravagance of Meenila's personal feelings towards her constituted an insuperable barrier.

Early in 1963 our friend the Rev. Joe Mullins, through whom years before Meenila had first been led to the Lord, paid us another visit. Once again he took a series of meetings for the younger children. Meenila was now nearly seventeen, but she had a great desire to hear this speaker again. Accordingly, when the evening meetings were in progress she would take up her position outside the House of Prayer where she could hear what was going on, without being seen. Mr. Mullins' talks were based on *The Pilgrim's Progress*, and once more God used him to meet her need. She went home one evening to record in her private note-book her new determination "to give myself wholly to the Lord".

She added as a rider to this resolve the significant statement "I must give up cinema songs".

She did this at once. The break was complete, and from that day onwards no one remembers ever hearing her sing one again.

Meenila's desire to give everything to the Lord was undoubtedly real and heartfelt, but the biggest thing that needed to be yielded to Him was her passion for her Accal which had become a form of idolatry. She could not experience true peace until the Lord was given the place that was His by right as the first and supreme object of her love and devotion.

The next few weeks were filled with emotional tension which reduced both the girl and the young woman to a state of exhaustion. Nesaruthina, wise and experienced as she was in Christian work, almost despaired of ever being able to help her charge. Meenila's craving for special attention got such a hold of her that she no longer had any control over it at all. The climax was reached on Easter Day. Early in the morning she made a scene. She was not, she declared, going to attend any of the traditional Easter services. Possibly she hoped her Accal would be afraid to leave her in such a state of agitation, and thus she would have her to herself while everyone else went off to the House of Prayer. To her surprise Nesaruthina simply left her. She wept and wailed hysterically but to no avail, no-one came back to pacify her.

Easter was holiday time. Nesaruthina had charge of quite a big group of boarding-school girls, and felt she could not possibly give them the help they needed if Meenila continued to play up in this way. Accordingly at her request the girl was moved away from her and the younger children and put to live among adults.

This disciplinary measure came to her as a terrific but salutary shock. A conscientious, trustworthy, hard-working girl who was ordinarily law-abiding, she had never for one moment imagined herself being publicly disgraced. Had she really let herself go to that extent?

She began to read her Bible again with the settled purpose of discovering and obeying God's will for her life. She did not have to seek Him long before He spoke to her. The verse He used startled her by its clear description of her state. It was Zephaniah 3 : 2. "She obeyed not the voice; she received not correction; she trusted not in the Lord; she drew not near to her God."

Now, when God Himself spoke to her with no human intervention at all, she was broken down. She turned to Him with her whole heart and asked for and received forgiveness for all that now, for the first time, she recognised as sin in her life. With this the Lord was enthroned in her heart. Instead of distressing emotional conflict she found peace.

Everyone saw the difference in her.

At the end of the holidays Meenila returned to her Accal again, but now the situation was transformed. There was no strain in their relationship. The Lord Jesus truly had first place, not only in Nesaruthina's life, but in Meenila's too.

Soon after this a well-loved senior Accal died. Her death was not unexpected, for she had been ill for many years and more acutely so for some months. Meenila was in no way disturbed by the news of her going, nor by the funeral service when she attended it, for now she had lost all fear of death. She even confided to one or two of those closest to her that she believed she would be the next to go to Heaven.

One day just a fortnight later she tidied her already tidy locker and, half jokingly, half seriously, said goodbye to some of her friends and to the children she had taught. She was apparently as well as usual, and they did not know what to make of her.

Late that afternoon she became suddenly ill, rapidly worsened, and went peacefully to be with the Lord the following day,

June 30th 1963, after less than twenty-four hours in hospital.

Within her short life Meenila had grappled with worse disappointments, had known fiercer conflict, and had faced bigger problems than had most of those around her. In the end she had found in Christ Jesus the answer to these problems and had experienced peace and joy in God her Saviour. Now, seeing His face, she was satisfied.

Her friends however are still with us. They are on the threshold of life with all its tremendous possibilities. Many of their crises still lie ahead of them. The humorist of Bala Stala days is now a trained nursery school teacher, while the bored baby is a lively young nurse who has revised her opinion on life and finds it good after all. Revathi is a secondary-grade teacher. One of the Pearls is working at the fibre industry in Pavilions. Usila is at Bangalore with the group employed in Jeya Toys, while shy, retiring Anihala achieved good results in school by her conscientious hard work and hopes to become a pharmacist. One or two of that group of babies about whose future I built castles in the air when I looked after them in my early days in Dohnavur have since failed to make the grade. With their education uncompleted, provision for their future will be difficult. But they are still young and their failure, though a real grief and sorrow, is a challenge to prayer and to further effort. Our God is still able to transform lives.

22

Reform

"Why on earth should these American professors be so interested in our village and our temple? I can't understand it."

The speaker was a tall, good-looking Brahman woman. Her home was in the small temple town where I had stayed to study Tamil, and where at festival time I had watched the *devadasis* dance. Now she was in hospital and had been telling me about a party of university men from the United States who were staying in the district and doing some research on Hinduism and Indian culture.

She was immensely interested in them and their customs. I wondered if they realised how their every action was observed and assessed by the charming women in whose homes they were sometimes entertained to a meal. My interrogator was exasperated because conversation on these occasions was always in English, which her husband talked well but which she did not understand.

"Even if the temple is very old, why should it be of interest to people who are not Hindus?" she asked. She was eager to talk, and told me more of the activities of these inexplicable strangers.

The professors had attended the festival. They had even helped pull the massive old wooden juggernaut car containing the god, which is dragged round the temple on the tenth day while people prostrate themselves in the dust before it. They were, it seemed, trying to get the "feel" of Hinduism from the inside. Their approach had greatly puzzled my informant who had seen nothing like it before.

"Did the *dasis* dance this year?" I asked. "You remember when I came and saw them about seventeen years ago."

My friend looked at me more in pity than in anger. "Didn't you know?" she asked. "All that was stopped by law years ago. The *dasis* were given a money allowance and they don't dance at all now."

Of course I had known about the legislation, but I was anxious to find out whether it had really been effective in so remote a spot as this town. My friend is an outspoken kind of person, and now in 1964 would, I believe, have told me quite frankly had the old ceremonies still been continuing under cover.

As long ago as 1947 there had been legislation limiting the activities of the *devadasis* and prohibiting the traffic in children which it entailed. This however had been a Madras State measure only. Seven years later in 1954 the whole question of the *devadasi* system and other allied social problems had come before the Central Government in Delhi. There had been much hot feeling on the subject and for a time the press daily published columns of conflicting views. Protagonists of the system declared that it kept alive a branch of India's most venerable art and culture. They affirmed that the singing and dancing of the temple girls was, too, an essential ingredient of Hindu worship. Its opponents deplored the subtle dangers of a practice in which religion indirectly gave sanction to prostitution and child traffic.

The Bill, which eventually passed into law, made it illegal for temple girls to sing and dance before the gods and at certain other public ceremonies. For women already employed in this way, and for their families, it made financial provision so that they were no longer compelled to practise their arts for a livelihood. The placing of this Act on the Statute Book was a notable victory for the social reformers, but of course in outlying districts it took some time to carry it fully into effect.

In 1955 a baby girl was sent to us by missionary friends. They told us she had been brought to their home by people who said they had found her pushed into a cactus hedge. The poor baby, obviously just newly born, was bleeding from scratches. If the missionaries did not want her, the finders said they would take her to the local temple. They seemed quite sure she would not be refused there. So it seemed that even at that late date the women of this particular temple were still prepared to train children for infamous purposes. Custom dies hard. But she was in fact the last baby we received about whom we had irrefutable evidence that, if we had not taken her, she would have been given to a temple.

One day in 1964 I was being shown by a friend round the great temple of Siva in a famous South Indian city. She had been magistrate of the children's court in the city for many years and knew a lot about the life of its underworld.

"Where is the place where the *devadasis* used to be 'married' to the god?" I asked.

"Oh," said my friend, "I can show you the place, but nothing of that kind happens now. It has been put a stop to completely." Such a statement of course raises a major question. Unquestionably a tremendous social reform has been achieved in recent years. Does this mean that there is no longer any need for the special kind of work for children we have been doing in Dohnavur? To this question my magistrate friend went on to suggest an answer.

She told me that in spite of the changed social climate she believed the moral danger to unprotected small children to be almost as great as it had ever been. What she said about the sources of this danger agreed very closely with what others in various official positions had also told us.

In India, as in the West, prostitution with its allied evils has not been ended by legislation. It has only gone underground. Here, as elsewhere, there are moral problems which defy all efforts made by the police and by social welfare organisations to eradicate them.

This Magistrate and the Vigilance Officers, and heads of Social Service departments in Madras whom we approached for information all told the same story of the continuance of traffic in little children ultimately destined for the brothels. They said that whereas the temples used only to take high caste children to be trained as *dasis*, women who procure children solely for purposes of immoral gain will accept those of any caste. They do nevertheless take into consideration the child's complexion and features, and they believe that "a noble child will have noble ways" and so be a better financial investment than one of humbler origins.

Children most likely to fall into such unscrupulous hands are of course babies born out of wedlock or those whose mother, or both parents, have died, but even quite responsible parents are known to dispose of an unwanted child.

Some years back one of our number found himself travelling in a railway carriage with two cultured Hindus, the Police Superintendent of our District and a local Member of the Madras Legislative Assembly. Asked by the latter, a Brahman, what kind of children were brought to our care in Dohnavur, he hesitated to refer to the *devadasi* system, then still active, and spoke instead of the sale of superfluous children to the cinema companies as described in an earlier chapter. When the Member expressed astonishment at this, the Superintendent of Police spoke up in support. "I have tried my hardest," he said, "to dissuade one of my head constables from doing just that with his daughter, entirely without success."

We have had children brought to us with a considerable price on their heads offered by women of evil repute. Of course we pay none. The Madras Social Workers told us that although this kind of transaction was usually hard to trace and to prove, their experience led them to believe it was not at all uncommon. When a criminal offence could be proved, they and the police could take action, but there was little or nothing they could do to prevent such offences from being committed. They encouraged us to continue in our work, which in their view had a real preventive value.

One afternoon a doctor friend arrived in Dohnavur looking very tired and bringing a beautiful little baby. She said she could not stay to rest but must be off again at once. She would not have left her own pressing affairs just then had she not felt it urgent to get the child to us. Some months earlier, she told me, a young unmarried Brahman girl of good family, whose father held an influential post, had consulted her with the request that she would terminate an unwanted pregnancy. The doctor had refused to do this. At length she heard that the baby had been born, and a day or two later she learned that a woman, known to have been in the courts for her immoral traffic in girls, was making offers for it. Realising what was afoot she dropped everything and went at once to see the girl and her parents. They were delighted to hear of a good home for the child, and willingly gave her to the doctor. For reasons of social prestige, and in consideration of the young mother's future prospects, they were determined to get rid of the baby quickly and unobtrusively. When so acceptable an alternative offered they were only too relieved however not to let the other woman have her.

This case confirmed a great deal of what our various informants had said. It showed too how much Christians in key positions can do to save children if they are alerted to the possible dangers and prepared for the sacrifice that may be involved. To intelligent, responsible Christians here in India it is perhaps impossible to overstate the urgency of this, for the needs are many and varied, and so therefore are the swiftly passing opportunities.

We heard recently how, in a neighbouring State, economic need has sometimes been terribly exploited for gain. In time of famine small girls are offered employment in a family in return for food, "care" and a small wage. The parents' anxiety is allayed by the payment of the first month's wage, and then the child may disappear, to be sold in the far away north into the home of a man probably diseased and dying, for there is a popular belief in that part of the country that a man can be cured of certain diseases by marriage with a very young girl. Naturally the child may seek escape from this situation, but to whom?

On all sides too we continue to hear Indians express the view that behind the cinema industry there lurk grave social evils. Very many boys and girls migrate to the big cities hoping to pick up a film part. Those girls who fail, or who get no more than a small temporary part, are likely to drift into prostitution. Government enquiry is resisted by the extremely powerful industry, and under existing legislation it is difficult for the police to act. It is estimated that ninety-nine per cent of the women who get small parts have some moral lapse before leaving cinema employ. A very high proportion of the girls admitted to the State vigilance homes come from this kind of life. What a challenge to Christian action!

There is one major difference today however. Those who participate in immoral practices and those who profit by them can no longer plead religious sanction for the trade. Constant efforts are now being made by the appropriate authorities to trace and deal

with them. Their activities are therefore driven further and
further underground, making it increasingly difficult to locate the
danger spots or to know when a particular child really needs the
kind of help that a work such as ours can give.

From about 1956 onwards our statistics showed a steady drop
in the numbers of new babies coming to us. In 1957 we had
twenty-three babies and little children brought to us. In the
following year the total was eleven and in 1959 it dropped to
only six. In the next two or three years we continued to receive
very few children.

We asked ourselves various questions. Assuming that the need
remained, was God no longer able to trust us with the care of
little ones? Had we failed in the task He had given us, or was He
purposely allowing us a respite from the continuous pressure so
that we might have time to set other parts of our house in order?
Was there more we should be doing to make the present danger
to children known to our Christian friends around us? It seemed
likely that some of them, impressed by the legislation banning
the *devadasi* system, had assumed that all was now well, that our
work was coming to an end, and that there was nothing further
for them to do in this matter.

At the end of 1963 and the beginning of 1964 we made these
questions a special matter of prayer, and asked our friends to join
with us in bringing this whole situation before God. We asked
Him to deal with the hold-up, whether the causes lay in ourselves or in external circumstances.

During the following months He gave us the joy of welcoming
into our nurseries eighteen new babies, three of whom were boys.
Since however the position with regard to child traffic seems to
grow more complex and difficult to elucidate as time passes, there
is still need to pray earnestly for unprotected children who run
the risk of being sold into an evil life.

23

Retrospect

It was Sunday, and most of us had been to the Tamil service in the House of Prayer. Now it was the girls' lunch time. Grace had been sung and the place of honour between Accal and a six-year-old, who had been celebrating her birthday, had been allotted to the guest. We were seated in a circle on the red-tiled floor of their cottage home. Steaming rice had been served from the large brass vessel which the children had carried over from the kitchen together with a bowl of curried vegetables, a crackling pile of crisp *appalam*, and a big bowl of buttermilk. Each child ate her lunch from a shining brass *kumba*, but as I was a guest mine had been served in traditional South Indian style on a plantain leaf. Against its green freshness the big pile of white rice before me, with the colourful portions of curry around it, looked very appetising indeed. Now as the meal progressed the children's temporary shyness rapidly disappeared, and conversation warmed up nicely.

"Sittie, I have just passed my second class Guide test." The

speaker's shining eyes proclaimed her an enthusiast. About eleven
years old, she was one of the older girls in the room, a thriving
healthy schoolgirl. Yet it would be hard to imagine a more
pathetic little scrap of humanity than she had been when she first
came to us. It was good to see her wholesome out-going attitude
now. Guiding had certainly helped to develop independence and
initiative in her.

"I had to cook a meal, and bath and dress a baby," she continued. The three-year-old member of the family who had
evidently been "guinea-pig" for the necessary practice in this
latter skill looked none the worse for the experience.

"There was a kind of seed inside the stone," announced the
six-year-old irrelevantly. Oblivious of the discussion going on
around her she was pursuing a deeply interesting line of thought
of her own. "And now there is a root," she added.

"We've got a banana tree over there." "And a papaya." "And
did you notice our chilli plants?" There was an animated chorus
at this point on the theme of their gardening experiments and
successes.

A lull followed and the youngest member seized the opportunity for which she had evidently been waiting. It was Sunday
and obviously Sittie ought to be told a Bible story. All this talk
of fruit trees and gardens suggested to her a suitable one.

"Eve picked the fruit," she stated, with fitting solemnity, "and
she ate it."

"We are doing Acts in school this term," contributed a thirteen-
year-old, the oldest girl present. "The subject is witness, and we
have been studying Paul's life."

It was all very disjointed but clearly the teaching had been on
the right wave-length and had got across.

Now some of the bigger girls were anxious to discuss something
else.

"We have our Current Events class on Tuesdays. Did you know about the cyclone? A train was crossing the bridge at Danushkodi and an enormous wave came and the train was turned upside down in the water." This was a fairly accurate summary of the first published version of this disaster and was a sobering piece of information. In the quiet that followed the baby saw her chance to continue imparting Bible instruction. Now Naaman and his leprosy were the subject of her lesson.

"How did he bathe?" asked one of the older girls, anxious that the extent of her little sister's accomplishments should be fully appreciated.

"He bathed like this," was the reply, and earnestly holding her nose with her small thumb and forefinger, she ducked. "One . . . two . . . three . . ." she continued, "and after the seventh time his skin was just like the new baby in Kairava Accal's house."

"Sittie, what happened to Madi Ammal?" asked an older child. She had been allowed to come to hospital at Christmas time to see the leprosy patients have their feast. Some of the food for this had been voluntarily contributed by the children and so a selected few of them came to see the recipients of their gift enjoying it, and to report to the others on what they had seen. This girl had been very touched by an abjectly poor patient whom she had noticed among the others. The unfortunate woman has lost her sight as a result of her disease. Her hands and feet too are badly deformed.

For a few moments conversation centred around the leprosy patients, and then the three-year-old chimed in again. She was determined to demonstrate her repertoire of stories. This time she had somehow got Jonah inside the big fish and was intent on getting him to safety again. Her baby Tamil is sometimes difficult for the uninitiated to follow but she makes up for this with her histrionic gifts. On this occasion there was no difficulty in getting her meaning.

The young Accal in charge proceeded tranquilly with her meal. She had the situation well in hand and there was no need for her to talk much. It was clear there is a good understanding between her and her children, and the family gave the impression of being contented and happy. Their ages range from three to thirteen, and all eight of them effervesce with life and good spirits.

How much there was to cheer and encourage as I thought over some of the subjects suggested by that brief lunch-time encounter! We have prayed often and earnestly for fellow-workers to be given to us from among our own children. That day I had seen one such in action, one out of many.

We can never be grateful enough for those of the older generations who have given long years of faithful service, without ever having had the interest and excitement of professional training in the wider world that these have today. They must now watch much younger people enjoying opportunities and gaining experience denied to them. It is the grace of the Lord that enables them to continue to give themselves ungrudgingly in the tasks that have engaged them for so long.

Circumstances have greatly changed. Today our young people grow up with far wider choices before them than their seniors ever had. We have sometimes wondered whether from among them recruits would ever be found who would be willing to work on the same self-sacrificing terms. There is so much to draw them elsewhere, and nothing but the constraining love of God to bring them back here. Would any of them respond to this so otherworldly constraint?

In many, God's compelling love has proved sufficient. We have now between twenty and thirty women (my young lunch-time hostess described above is among them) whose training and experience would ensure them security and independence in the world, but who have chosen to return to work here for the Lord's sake. This gives us confidence that, as we continue to pray, others with like qualifications will hear and obey His voice when He calls.

It was good to know that the three-year-old expert in Old Testament History, the enthusiastic Girl Guide, the eager gardeners, the follower of Current Events and the one concerned for the leprosy patient would remain (if all goes according to plan) with the same Accal and with each other until the end of their schooldays.

The change-over from sets of all one age-group to family groups of mixed ages is one of the major achievements of the past years. The agony of being changed at a given age from one Accal's care to that of another is being slowly eliminated. They now stay with a single Accal from the time they leave the tiny babies' nursery until they pass out of school into a more adult world. This arrangement approximates far more nearly to a normal family life.

By the time the children of Meenila's set were eight or nine years old we were already working towards the provision of a more stable home background. Even so she herself passed through the hands of five different Accals and suffered emotionally with each change. Had she come to Dohnavur a few years earlier she might have experienced even more such moves.

When the Family was much smaller and Amma was in a very real sense mother to all the children, these changes did not matter nearly so much. Everyone had free and frequent access to her. It was her love and understanding and the stability of their relationship with her that gave them security.

With the Family as large as it has become, it is out of the question for any one person to know every child intimately. They must find their security in a stable, loving relationship with someone within their own smaller circle. The obvious person to provide this is the Accal who looks after them. A child cannot form a significant affection for an indefinite number of people. If too many attempts to do so are made the end result is liable to be superficiality in all human relationships and an unstable, immature character.

Now that we ask anyone who comes back to Dohnavur with the aim of looking after children to be prepared to do it on a comprehensive and long-term basis, it is of paramount importance that each one shall be sure of her call. If she leaves her children after she has really won their confidence and welded them into a family group the effects of the disrupted relationship go very deep and leave scars that may be permanent. Still more is this so if we mistakenly accept someone for service who is not spiritually ready for it and who subsequently has to be relieved of this responsibility, or even asked to leave altogether.

My lunch party was with a group of girls, but something should also be said about the boys. As has already been explained, the small boys are cared for by Accals until they are about eight, when they move to live with the older boys and men and come under the care of Annachies. Most changes of Accal in the early years have been eliminated for them, as for the girls. In the boys' part of the Family it has long been the aim for one Annachie to take his set of boys right through until they leave school. The one outstanding deficiency in this system however is the lack of feminine care and affection in their homes (and the courtesies that this calls for in response) during the school years. It is Rajappan and Nuranie, and the one or two other married couples who have volunteered to follow their lead, as described in Chapter 20, who have pioneered the way towards remedying this. Theirs is however but a small beginning as yet.

Another change within the Family which was introduced almost concurrently with the new home arrangements concerned dress.

For many years our children had worn uniform. Home-woven, hard-wearing cotton in gay, tasteful colours, it varied from age-group to age-group and was bright and attractive, but "different" in a subtle way from the clothes of other children in the villages around us. Away at boarding school it simply would not have done, and less conspicuous dress was essential there.

Eventually in the late 1950s we decided to abandon uniform altogether, except for special occasions which, at the Family's own request, include Sunday services. Ordinarily the children now wear the same varied assortment of styles and colours as are to be seen in any South Indian village.

Thus we had sat together that lunch time in our traditional Sunday best. As I am a doctor the children who entertained me had talked quite a lot about the hospital and the leprosy patients. Inexperienced as they were their imaginations had been stirred by that great crowd of maimed, poverty-stricken people enjoying their Christmas feast. They wanted to know more about them, and more about the other work of the hospital too, so that they could pray more understandingly. For the Place of Heavenly Healing is still a door of opportunity and there is much to tell.

24

Changing Outlook, Unchanging Challenge

The hospital had continued through the years to provide the Family with its first evangelistic field.

From 1956 to 1961 the medical work boomed. Annual out-patient attendances topped the forty-five thousand mark, and in some years there were more than three thousand in-patient admissions. Our patients were drawn from a wide area. Hindus, Christians and Muslims continued to come. We contacted people of all types and of many different opinions, and made a lot of friends.

Changes within the Family however began to have their reper-cussions on our staff situation. Each year a few school-leavers opt for a nursing or para-medical training. We receive them into our hospital and give them some preliminary tuition and experience in nursing or dispensing for perhaps one or two years. Then, just as they are becoming really useful, we have to send them on to other hospitals in order that they may qualify for and take their State Examinations. So far most of the girls who have completed their training have subsequently married or have taken employment elsewhere. We have had fewer recruits from among them than we had hoped for and expected.

During the last few years some of the senior members of our home-trained and missionary staff have retired. Failing health and strength have compelled others to reduce their quota of work.

By 1962 we found ourselves left with a staff quite inadequate to deal with the volume of work that almost overwhelmed us. Our first aim is to demonstrate the love of God to our patients, and to make sure that they individually understand its personal implications. For this we need more personnel than do hospitals which deal with medical treatment only, or which rely on professional full-time evangelists for the spiritual side of the work. If our staff members are to lead people to Christ, they must have time to get alongside the patients, to enter into their lives, to sympathise with them in their troubles, to read the Bible with them and to introduce them to the Lord Jesus when they are ready to meet Him.

Reluctantly we decided that in order to meet our evangelistic obligations with the staff available we would have to cut down some of our medical work. It was simply a question of needs must. After much prayer, planning and experiment, and with very conflicting emotions, we reduced our bed-strength and set an approximate limit to the number of out-patients we should see each day. Staffing difficulties have always been most acute on the men's side of the work, and once again we found ourselves obliged to reduce this to an absolute minimum.

There was a time, especially during the war years, when we were offering virtually the only accessible medical service of comparative quality in the area. Today, patients to whom we are compelled to refuse treatment should generally be able to get help elsewhere. Government medical services have been very much extended, though they are still inadequate for the enormous population of the country. In this district, for instance, there is still almost no Government-sponsored provision for leprosy patients.

Knowing this we thought we might try to extend our leprosy work. There seemed a real need for such a work locally, and with modern sulphone treatment much can be achieved with no great outlay in staff and facilities. Instead of leaving the men's wards empty, we decided we would use them for leprosy cases needing minor surgical or major medical help. We made a survey, albeit a very amateur and incomplete one, of some of the areas from which our patients come, and found quite a number of new leprosy cases. Word got around that we were interested in treating the disease, and our clinics, both for men and women, grew by leaps and bounds. They are still increasing. These people, many of them maimed, disfigured and desperately poor, unwanted even by their own families, are often very ready to hear about a God who loves and cares for them. Several among them have definitely put their trust in Him. To visit the leprosy ward and find some of them deeply engrossed in Bible study is one of our great joys.

God has blessed the steps we took with the interests of His kingdom in view. In the last year or two He has allowed us to see more of our patients turning to Him than in the previous few years of greater medical pressure.

Village evangelism also continues, and in very many cases the people who welcome teaching are those whose first introduction to Christianity was made in the wards of our hospital. But whether in these wards or elsewhere, our evangelistic work is now done against a background very different from that of eighteen or twenty years ago. It is a background of paradox and contradiction, of revolutionary changes running alongside conservative adherence to ancient customs.

Outwardly the villages are transformed in many respects. There are electric lights in the streets, in the shops, even in some of the houses. Other houses are still merely one-roomed mud-and-thatch hovels, where life subsists at the lowest level of poverty and deprivation. Most villages now have their powered rice mill, and women take their grain there to be milled instead of laboriously dehusking it by hand. On many wells electric pumps have super-seded primitive bucket-and-sleeve water-lifts for irrigation. Nearly every village has its communal radio, and many people have sets of their own as well. By contrast, in most rural areas elementary sanitation is still a rare luxury. But roads and com-munications generally are much improved. Eighteen years ago about three buses came each day down the branch road to the hospital. Now there are thirty.

Many people travel. While sitting on the floor in some sparsely furnished village house, one may be drawn surprisingly into a discussion of the relative merits of sea and air travel by a woman who has experienced both.

Literacy has increased and people are reading. They are be-coming more aware of national and international events. Thoughts and opinions far removed from local tradition are making an impact in unlikely places. Christian theological students are reading *Honest to God*, and country pastors are making their assess-ment of the "New Theology". Writing about missionaries of the last century a Hindu author, Professor T. P. Meenakshisundaran, makes a two-edged comparison. "Their acceptance of the myth-ology of the Bible as authentic history . . . is naïve, and this gives a picture of the West different from what we know of it in this century." Our evangelistic problems do not all originate in the East!

Led by Dr. S. Radhakrishnan, India's President, whose writings are widely popular, there is a renascence of Hinduism, but by the intellectuals it is now largely de-mythologised. It is also increasingly eclectic, and its modern thinkers and writers willingly incorporate a substantial percentage of Christian ethical teaching into their own philosophy. Many are prepared to venerate and worship Christ as one of the many manifestations of the Supreme Being. "The same God is worshipped by all." So writes Dr. Radhakrishnan. "The differences of conception and approach are determined by local colouring and social adaptations. All manifestations belong to the same Supreme . . . God is the rewarder of all who diligently seek Him whatever views of God they may hold. The spiritually immature are unwilling to recognise other gods than their own. Their attachment to their creed makes them blind to the larger unity of the God-head. This is the result of egotism in the domain of religious ideas."* In these days many of the educated people of South India would agree with these sentiments. The one thing they cannot abide is the "intolerance" that claims that Jesus is Himself supreme and unique, that He, with the Father and the Spirit, is alone worthy of worship, and that in no other name is there salvation.

Some more militant Hindu sects and organisations are aggressively missionary. Others are philanthropic and provide excellent social services. An entirely new form of congregational liturgical worship, in which women take part, is being brought into use in the temples. In some places the Hindu holy books are expounded at length over a public address system in the evenings and far into the night. Many shrines and temples have been extensively restored. This is not only because of their religious significance, but also because they are a part of the nation's heritage and symbols of its solidarity. For Hinduism transcends language and State barriers, and so is exploited as a means to national unity.

* S. Radhakrishnan, *The Bhagavadgita*, London, George Allen & Unwin, 1948, pp. 159f.

Islam, though a minority faith, still holds its followers in a relentless and fanatical grip as it has done for centuries. The Gospel cannot be said yet to have made significant inroads into this stronghold.

Materialism and communism are exercising an increasingly strong influence. This is especially so in the large industrial cities and the universities, but their influence is felt even in remote country districts.

In spite of all this, a considerable number of the patients who come to our hospital still hold the beliefs, customs and traditions of their ancestors. These include a strong underlay of pre-Aryan Animism which pervades this largely Dravidian area and exerts, through allegiance to local village gods, goddesses and demons, a strong influence particularly on women. We still encounter from time to time a tremendous barrier of primitive superstition, prejudice, and even stark fear.

Conversely, people are much more sophisticated than they were a few years ago. When some years back we first took a gramophone and played Tamil records prepared by Gospel Recordings in a sleepy agricultural village not far from here, the children of one of the land-owners gathered in open-mouthed amazement and asked, "*Where* is the man who is singing? Is he really small enough to get inside that box?" Today those same children have a radio in their house along with various other modern gadgets. Sponsored by the Block Development Officer and partially subsidised by the Government, their father has launched a radio and furniture factory in a nearby town with a branch factory in his own village.

For years old-fashioned lantern slides projected on to a white-washed wall used to guarantee an interested audience for the Gospel talk they illustrated. Now the cinema-going youth is blasé and critical even of our more contemporary still transparencies. "They showed a dumb cinema last night and it didn't have a single woman in it," was the verdict of a six-year-old who had seen one such effort.

New philosophy, new theology, new morality, new scientific know-how, new amenities of all kinds, new styles in dress, new tastes in food, new amusements, all these things abound. Yet the human heart remains unsatisfied. Neither the wholesale scepticism of the intellectuals nor the undiscriminating credulity of the ignorant lead to peace. Christ is still the only answer.

How are the thousands of people around us to come to know Him? How can we reach with the Gospel the illiterate mother and her graduate sons and daughters; the caste-bound old widow and her emancipated, progressive grandchildren; the devout Muslim and the careless nominal Christian?

Since even in this modern age the flesh is heir to many ills from which it seeks relief, a hospital is a rendezvous for people of all sorts and conditions. A Christian hospital affords unprecedented opportunities for making known the Good News to folk who would otherwise never hear it.

The nurses, dispensers and others whom God has been using in the past to buy up these opportunities are now getting on in years. One or two of them are seriously unfit and will be unable to continue much longer in the work they have loved so well. Who will take their place? Who will respond to the challenge of the tremendous need and the constant wonderful opportunity?

25

Cheerfully to Continue

It was high noon on May 15th 1964. The heat of the sun-baked road scorched our feet. The dazzling glare drove our little group to refuge in the meagre shade of the banyan tree that year by year reaches further out over the hospital wall. No-one talked very much as we waited there. We were all busy with our own thoughts, and some of us were having a struggle to keep our feelings under control. Suddenly a cloud of reddish dust and the glint of sunlight on silver paint and windscreen heralded the arrival of the Family car. In a moment it was alongside. There was just time, as it paused there, for us to call our goodbyes. Then it was off again round a corner in the road and out of sight.

May Powell had left us. We could hardly credit the evidence of our eyes that she had really gone. She was the latest of a long line of those who, having "finished their course" of service here, had at last retired.

May had joined the Fellowship in 1924 and her life had been inextricably linked with that of the Family ever since. Inevitably therefore her going marked for us a big break with our past. Inevitably too there was sadness at the parting. We were losing a dearly loved human leader, but we had the assurance that our Unseen Leader was still with us, unchanging and entirely sufficient.

If May's going marked the end of a phase of the Family's history, it also witnessed the answers to many prayers, the fulfilment of many hopes and the start of a number of new and most promising projects.

Four or five years earlier a plan had been mooted for beginning a permanent hostel for young men at some place away from Dohnavur. There is often a waiting period between their leaving school and securing entry to training or obtaining permanent employment. This hiatus in their career occurs just at a stage when their overflowing energies badly need to be directed into profitable channels. It was hoped that such a hostel might afford a means of usefully bridging this gap. The lads would work at some industry, or on an agricultural project, and so start to earn something towards their keep. In a small group they could be brought into closer touch with ordinary town or village life while still having the help of one of their own Annachies.

It proved surprisingly difficult to find a site for the hostel at a reasonable price, and the plan was delayed because of this. Then, early in 1964 and after much journeying and many fruitless enquiries, Thyaharaj came upon exactly the right piece of land. Near the town of Cheranmahadevi (formerly Shermadevi) and only seventeen miles from Dohnavur, it is ideal for agricultural development. Legal formalities were completed and the land was bought. In May 1964 a service of dedication was held and the work of building begun. Anandavanam was a reality. When I saw it at this stage it looked to me as if we had bought a substantial tract of thorny desert. But the experts were right: it has proved to be good fertile land, ripe for development.

In the same eventful month Eleanor Backhouse set out on a new venture, a two thousand mile journey to the extreme north of the country. Her destination was Dharamsala in Uttar Pradesh, the seat of the Tibetan government in exile. Missionary friends there had negotiated for her to be granted interviews with key Tibetan officials and she also had the privilege of an audience with the Dalai Lama and his sister. The knowledgeable intervention of these same friends led to the selection of six teen-age Tibetan girls to accompany her back to Dohnavur.

Some time previously missionaries from North India who had interested themselves in the Tibetan refugees had told us of their terribly crowded settlements and inadequate educational facilities. The Dalai Lama and his ministers were glad, they said, to accept, on behalf of their young people, offers of temporary accommodation, education and any form of training likely to be of use to the Tibetan people of the future. Our friends had tentatively asked whether we might consider giving some help along these lines.

We had thought and prayed about the suggestion. We could offer some English-medium education and give training in child-care and elementary nursing. We could also provide a loving home. If such a project had God's sanction and approval, might He not use it far more widely than just for the help of a few teen-age refugees? We were gripped and stimulated by a vision of the possibilities.

Now in this month of May 1964 the new venture was no mere dream. As May Powell said her goodbyes and set off to join her ship, the plan was well on the way to fulfilment.

From the rail-head at Tirunelveli May's train was to follow in reverse the route described at the outset of this book by which, eighteen years earlier, I had entered India and first reached Dohnavur. All the way northward through Madura and Trichy to Madras, then on through Andhra Pradesh and up across the Deccan plateau to Bombay, she met with a succession of brief but·joyous reunions and fond farewells. At every possible point on that. thousand-mile journey she encountered Old Boys and Old Girls of the Family, eager as ever to hear the latest news of home and determined above all to say their loving goodbyes to her in person. Some of them had taken a day off from work, thus curtailing their precious annual leave. Others had locked up their houses, and complete with babies and small children had trailed off to some crowded station where her train must stop and so provide the opportunity for a few precious minutes of conversation. Here was proof, if proof were needed, of the good hand of God upon our efforts to ease the way of our young men and women out into the world of competitive employment, wherever they can find scope for their gifts and energies. And it would have been the same had her journey taken her to Calcutta or to Delhi, for they are dispersed throughout India from Cape Comorin in the south to the Punjab in the far north.

Every holiday time sees crowds of them back home again on visits, and indeed there must be few days in the year when no Old Boy or Old Girl is here. Never a day passes without bringing letters from some of them. They write asking for advice or requesting help of various kinds, or just to share with us the news of their lives and families; and scarcely one letter concludes without asking for our continued prayers. What a challenge to us is this recurring appeal!

Of this far-flung family some are successful men and women in the professions, others are humble workers in village centres; some are in industry or the armed Defence Forces, while others are struggling along in domestic service. Some of them have dedicated their whole lives to the work of God's Kingdom as evangelists or pastors, as helpers in homes for destitute children or the old and disabled, or as staff members of various Christian institutions. There are others who are just as definitely serving the Master in secular employment. Some of our married girls are using their homes as a base from which to witness for Christ to their neighbours and are taking an active part in the life and work of the churches they have joined. Every one who is thus committed to the Lord for His service is a cause to us of joy and thanksgiving. Backed by our prayers, what could they not accomplish for Him in this their own great land of India?

But it would be entirely false to suggest that all are a joy to us. Some have chosen to leave God out of their lives. Some have become deeply entangled in sin and have as yet found no way back to liberty. Some, too, are embittered and sadly estranged from us. All these cause us anxiety and sorrow; but they surely need our love and our prayers even more than do the former. We may temporarily have lost touch with them, but God has not. Still today He has the power to liberate and transform and renew them.

Back here in Dohnavur we were, by that spring of 1964, seeing the answer to many prayers in the increasingly large and valuable contribution being made to the work by our Indian brothers and sisters. God has so worked that the Indian leadership which seemed far off in 1949, and for which we had prayerfully toiled for many years, is now in many parts of our Family an accomplished fact. Membership of the Fellowship is now almost equally divided between Indians and Europeans. Of the fifteen members of the Council, nine are Indian. We do not strive to appoint Indians just because of their race. The criterion is: who, in God's eyes, is the best person to undertake such responsibility as it arises. This is the way He has led us and blessed us.

As our story will have shown, the Leadership Group has undergone various changes since its inception. Philip England has succeeded John Risk in co-leadership, with Margaret Wilkinson as May Powell's successor in the same role. Purripu Sargunam has retired. The other members of the group are Rajappan, Thyaharaj, David Aruldasan, his sister Shanthie and Eleanor Backhouse.

There is indeed very much for which to thank God who has so manifestly led us through these years. There is very much too that challenges us in the immensely enlarged sphere of our witness and potential influence. Entirely new avenues of service have been opened up for us in Bangalore, in villages in the north of Tirunelveli District, and in Cheranmahadevi. Our widely dispersed Family now makes an impact for good or ill far byond the confines of our locality, or even of the Tamil-nad. The young people flowing out in a constant stream from Dohnavur must inevitably make their presence felt in the places where they settle. We are thus responsible for preparing them, during the impressionable years of their childhood and adolescence, for life and witness in a far wider setting than was formerly envisaged.

God has used the medical work of the hospital to win us friends in countless towns and villages around us. A welcome such as we hardly dared hope for in former years now awaits any from here who go to those towns bearing to their folk the good news of a Saviour who loves them.

But there is another aspect to this. Not only are there more evangelistic opportunities; there are also far more people to be evangelised. By statistics in the daily press and by the uninhibited publicity of the Government's family planning campaign, we are constantly reminded of India's exploding population. Even now the hard fact of food rationing warns of problems ahead in the production of sufficient staple foodstuffs. But disturbing as the population explosion must be to social and economic planners, it should be even more disturbing to messengers of the Gospel, for it means that far more people in our area will die without ever hearing of Christ unless we can find ways of telling them.

As we take sober stock of our situation there is no room for complacency. The work has grown, there is a rich harvest ripe for reaping, but workers are pathetically few. Even with the welcome addition of many new Indian colleagues, the retirement of overseas workers due to age and other reasons has so depleted our strength that the Fellowship is now far smaller numerically than it was twenty years ago. The hospital and boys' work are seriously understaffed. Wherever we look we see things that we long to do abandoned for want of personnel. We are not keeping pace with the growing opportunities, and they may never come again.

The world situation too, with its wars, its bitter inter-racial strife, its strong ideological and nationalistic movements, suggests that we may be working against time. The door of opportunity may not remain open much longer.

How should we meet this situation? Is it unreasonable to think that God can still supply our need of people just as surely as He has supplied our material and spiritual needs? The experiences of the years have given us ample ground for believing that He can. While He still leads us on, would it not rather be unreasonable therefore to refuse to go forward?

Certainly nothing less than God's constraining love can suffice to bring young people from the luxury of the West and the security of a welfare state to come and help in so seemingly precarious a venture. But be assured that it is no whit easier for young people in this country to abandon their prospects of advancement and success, in a world where these may be the only alternative to abject poverty, in favour of service which must often seem circumscribed and wearisome, and, what is worse, perilously insecure.

Many years back Amma faced a not dissimilar situation. She tells of it in one of the last chapters of *Gold Cord* "Spare not;

lengthen the cords and strengthen the stakes," had seemed to be
the word that had come from the Lord Himself. "Yet we knew,"
she wrote, "how far we were from doing thoroughly all that
should be done; and superficial work is pretence of the worst sort.
How then attempt more?"

The work had grown; yet no possible recruits were in view to
help sustain it. Current income had exceeded expenditure only
by a fantastically small margin—less in fact, than one shilling in
five thousand pounds. (This was a trial of faith God has not called
us to face at present.) Already India was restive. It was 1931, with
Mahatma Gandhi attending the Round Table Conference in
London to plead for Indian independence, only to be jailed within
a week of his return to this country. Surely this was no time to
embark on new ventures costly in personnel and money.

Yet to attempt more was exactly the challenge she and her
colleagues were then facing. They did therefore what they were
accustomed to do. They spent a day in united prayer, facing
together the challenge of the uncompleted task. The end of that
day found them triumphantly singing:

> Lord God of doors we cannot pass,
> We go where Thou art leading on.

The decision that emerged was not the expected one, to retrench.
It was the improbable, the unreasonable one: they would go
forward in spite of appearances, confident in an all-sufficient God.

The God of yesterday is still today the unchanging and faithful
God. To Him who down the years has called men and women into
His service, to do so again is no problem. We too therefore, *not
forgetting to sing*, would press confidently on, free of all fears
concerning a morrow that is committed to His sure hands.

DATE DUE			
NOV 23 '7	NOV 5 '80	MAY 3 0 '01	
DEC 8 '7	DEC 2 '80		
FEB 4 '7	DEC 12 '80		
MAR 19 '73	APR 4 '84		
MAR 2 2 '73	MAY 30 '84		
OCT 12 '7	FEB 1 2 1986		
	MAY 1		
JAN 23 '7			
	NOV 20		
APR 3 '78	MAR 3 0 '93		
MAR 7 '80	MAY 4 4 '99		

GAYLORD M-2   PRINTED IN U.S.A.